Elara Merritt

Dark Femme Mastery

How to Become Magnetic, Desired, and Unforgettable Without Chasing Anyone

The Hidden Architecture

She stopped chasing, and the world began to follow.

Table of Contents

Introduction. You Were Never Meant to Be Tamed

The Myth of the Good Girl

You were never meant to be small.

You were never meant to be silent, soft in the wrong ways, agreeable at your own expense. And yet, somewhere along the line, you were taught to trade your fire for approval, your truth for politeness, your voice for safety.

The "good girl" myth is one of the most insidious programs ever embedded into the feminine psyche. It doesn't shout. It whispers. It comes wrapped in smiles, praise, and conditional love. It tells you to sit pretty, speak when spoken to, and be kind even when it costs you your self-respect. And worst of all, it convinces you that playing by those rules will earn you love, admiration, and protection.

But it never does.

The good girl is rewarded with exhaustion, invisibility, and a gnawing sense that no matter how much she gives, it's never quite enough.

This chapter is a reclamation. Not of rebellion for rebellion's sake, but of truth. Because the good girl is not real. She is a mask — one that must be removed if you are ever to access the deeper layers of your feminine power.

Where the Myth Began

Most of us don't choose to be the good girl. We're raised into her. Conditioned to believe that femininity equals obedience, sweetness, and sacrifice. From fairy tales to family dinners, the messaging is clear: be beautiful but not vain, intelligent but not intimidating, sensual but not sexual, caring but never confrontational.

You're taught to read the room before you speak. You're taught to make yourself smaller so others feel comfortable. And if you break the script — if you cry too loudly, speak too boldly, want too deeply — you're punished. Not always with direct criticism, but often with subtle cues: a frown, a withdrawal of affection, a look that says *you've gone too far.*

This is how the myth survives. Not because it's true, but because it's familiar.

The Hidden Cost of Goodness

The good girl isn't just emotionally stifled. She is energetically disempowered. By constantly seeking validation, she gives away her sovereignty. By prioritizing harmony at all costs, she disconnects from her own inner chaos — the very force that births true creation, seduction, and magnetism.

And here's the truth most won't tell you: power and "goodness" rarely coexist in the same form. Not the kind of goodness that's been sold to women. Because that goodness is docility dressed up as virtue. It's compliance mistaken for integrity.

The woman who embodies true feminine power does not aim to be good. She aims to be whole. She does not fear being too much — she fears being edited.

So ask yourself this: what has pretending to be good actually given you?

When you dimmed your voice, did they finally listen?

When you swallowed your no, did it make them love you more?

When you overgave, did it make you feel safer?

The answers don't lie in theory. They lie in your lived experience.

And if you're honest, you already know.

You know that being the good girl didn't make you magnetic. It made you invisible.

It didn't protect you. It made you prey.

The very things you were told would make you worthy — being quiet, sweet, soft — are the very things that silenced your instinct, suppressed your magnetism, and stole your edge.

This is not your failure. It's the design of the myth itself.

And here is where we begin to dismantle it.

But if the good girl is a lie, what replaces her? That's the fear that keeps many women clinging to her. Without her smile, her pleasing tone, her carefully measured reactions — who are you? What if you become hard, bitter, or unloved?

This fear is a clever trick. It keeps you orbiting someone else's center, always reacting, never leading. It convinces you that without your performance of goodness, you'll be discarded. But the truth is this: what you lose when you drop the good girl mask was never real love, safety, or worth to begin with. It was conditional attention, based on your ability to self-abandon convincingly.

What you gain, instead, is real power. Not power over others, but power over your own energy, your own choices, your own voice. A woman who is no longer addicted to being liked becomes dangerous to a system that profits from her self-doubt. That's why this myth is so persistent — because a woman who reclaims her full expression becomes unpredictable. And unpredictable women cannot be controlled.

You don't reclaim yourself all at once. It starts in small moments. Saying no without apology. Leaving messages unanswered because your energy matters. Wearing what makes you feel electric rather than palatable. Speaking up even when your voice shakes, or walking away even when someone tells you you're overreacting.

These aren't acts of rebellion. They are acts of return. Every time you refuse to shrink, you remember a little more of who you were before the programming took hold. And with each act of remembering, you become more magnetic.

There is nothing more compelling than a woman who doesn't need validation to feel whole. The world feels her before she enters the room. She's not loud. She doesn't beg. She doesn't chase. She simply *is* — full-spectrum, emotionally honest, willing to take up space without asking for permission.

She is not perfect. She is powerful. She is not always kind. She is always true. And because of that, she is unforgettable.

You do not become this woman by adding layers. You become her by stripping away what was never you. The silence. The guilt. The compulsion to perform softness while suffocating in silence. You peel away the fear of being too much, too angry, too sensual, too loud, too wild — and underneath it, you find someone who was always waiting to be let out.

This is your invitation to let her out.

Not tomorrow. Not when you've healed enough. Now.

The myth of the good girl will keep whispering. It will say, "Don't ruin the moment," "Don't upset him," "Don't speak up here." Let it whisper. Let it try. And then let it fail.

You were not born to be agreeable. You were born to remember. To reclaim. To become. And that journey begins the moment you stop trying to be good and start choosing to be real.

The world doesn't need more obedient women. It needs more women who are awake, electric, and unwilling to play roles that erase them. Let this be the last chapter you read through the lens of who you were trained to be. From here forward, read as the woman you were born to become.

The Forbidden Power of the Dark Feminine

There is a part of you that has always known. Even before you could name it, even before you dared to believe it, something inside whispered that your softness alone was never the whole story. That beneath the surface of grace and sweetness lived another force entirely. One that didn't ask. One that didn't beg. One that *knew*.

This is the dark feminine.

Not dark as in evil, but dark as in hidden. Suppressed. Misunderstood. It is the part of you that does not seek permission. The part that holds rage without apology, desire without shame, seduction without manipulation, and truth without dilution.

The dark feminine is not the opposite of the light feminine. It is her completion.

While the light embodies nurturing, compassion, surrender, and radiance, the dark is where boundaries are forged, intuition sharpens, seduction lives, and raw creation begins. She is the one who walks away without looking back. She is the one who chooses herself first. She is the one who burns the bridge *because she can build a better one alone*.

This power has always been yours. But you were trained to fear it.

From the earliest myths, dark feminine figures have been twisted into monsters. Lilith was demonized for refusing submission. Medusa was cursed for her uncontainable power. Kali was called dangerous, her destruction misunderstood. The pattern is consistent: when a woman refuses to be tamed, she is framed as threatening.

And in truth, she is. But not in the way they want you to believe.

She is threatening to systems that rely on your silence. She is threatening to relationships built on your self-sacrifice. She is threatening to anyone who benefits from your inability to see your worth without external reflection.

That is why this power has been hidden. Not because it is harmful. But because it is liberating.

To awaken your dark feminine is to reclaim your wholeness. It is to remember that you are not here to be palatable. You are not here to be praised for your politeness. You are here to embody all of you — the softness and the storm, the nurturing and the no, the glow and the gravity. But this reclamation does not happen by accident. It happens by choice.

It begins when you stop labeling your anger as a flaw and begin to see it as a compass. When you stop suppressing your desire and allow it to lead you toward what is alive. When you stop pretending that softness is your only value and recognize that your presence alone has the power to shift a room. The dark feminine is magnetic not because she tries to attract. She draws in what she wants by being fully attuned to herself. She doesn't chase. She doesn't convince. She simply *is* — fully, freely, and without dilution.

And that is her secret. She is not concerned with being liked. She is concerned with being aligned. And that alignment makes her unforgettable. You do not have to become someone else to access this. You only have to remove what was never you. The shame. The guilt. The fear of being too much or not enough. Beneath it all, the power is already waiting.

You've felt it before — in the moments you stood your ground, in the nights you chose yourself, in the decisions that made others uncomfortable but made you feel whole.

This is not about becoming dark for darkness's sake. It's about reclaiming the part of you that has been exiled. Because until you do, your power will always feel incomplete.

You don't step into this power by reading about it. You activate it by living it. The dark feminine doesn't emerge in theory. She rises in choice. In moments when you speak what has long been silenced, walk away when staying would be easier, or allow yourself to be seen without softening your edges to make others more comfortable.

She shows herself when you refuse to make yourself smaller just to be more digestible. When you allow others to feel intimidated, unsettled, or even rejected — not because you are cruel, but because you are no longer willing to betray yourself in order to be accepted.

This energy lives in the pause before you respond. It lives in your refusal to explain your no. It lives in your ability to hold both desire and detachment in the same breath. The dark feminine is not reactive. She is intentional. She does not scream to be heard. She waits, and in that stillness, she holds power others can't define or control.

You were taught to believe that this kind of power would make you lonely. That being too strong, too sensual, or too sovereign would scare people away. But you were never meant to attract the ones who only feel safe around your silence. You were meant to attract those who are drawn to your full spectrum — who don't just tolerate your intensity, but rise in response to it.

The dark feminine doesn't just change how others see you. She changes how you see yourself. She rewrites your inner dialogue. Where you once asked, "Is this too much?" you now ask, "Does this match my energy?" Where you once thought, "How can I make this work?" you now ask, "Is this even worthy of my presence?"

This shift is more than mindset. It is an energetic recalibration. You no longer need to contort yourself to gain approval, affection, or access. You become the source. You become the magnet. You become the field through which attraction, influence, and power are expressed.

But this embodiment comes with responsibility. The dark feminine is not reckless. She does not burn without purpose. Her chaos creates. Her silence speaks. Her movement is calculated not in fear, but in alignment. She knows that true power is not in domination, but in direction. She is not interested in controlling others. She is committed to controlling her own frequency.

And that is where her influence becomes undeniable.

People may not always understand her. They may call her intimidating, difficult, unpredictable. Let them. Let them try to categorize what refuses to fit. You are not here to be understood by everyone. You are here to remember what it feels like to be fully expressed.

This is the deeper truth: the world does not fear your darkness because it is harmful. It fears your darkness because it is free. And in that freedom, you become untouchable.

When you are no longer seeking to prove, perform, or please, you are no longer vulnerable to manipulation. You cannot be baited into overexplaining. You cannot be guilted into self-erasure. You cannot be convinced to abandon yourself to soothe someone else's discomfort.

The dark feminine is not a trend or aesthetic. It is not about dressing a certain way or speaking in hushed tones. It is the internal decision to no longer outsource your power. It is the choice to stop negotiating with your intuition. It is the path of embodiment, of shadow integration, of unapologetic presence.

You don't need to convince anyone of your worth. You only need to embody it. When you do, the energy you emit becomes undeniable. Some will fear it. Some will worship it. But most importantly, you will *feel* it — and you'll never be willing to dim it again.

This is not the beginning of something new. It is the return to something ancient. Something sacred. Something that has always been inside you, waiting to be remembered.

What This Book Will Do to You (and For You)

This book is not a how-to. It's not a set of polished steps meant to turn you into something that looks impressive on the outside but still feels hollow inside. It's not about following rules to become more lovable, more acceptable, more aligned with some external version of femininity.

This book is a weapon. A mirror. A flame.

It will challenge the parts of you that still seek approval. It will agitate the places in you that have grown numb from playing roles. It will speak to the version of you who has always known she was made for more, even if she's never had the words to explain why.

You won't find softness for the sake of being palatable. You won't be praised for staying quiet. You won't be taught to dilute your power under the guise of spiritual maturity or emotional regulation. This is not about balance. It's about awakening what's been buried and reclaiming what's been denied.

This book will meet you where you've been pretending to be less. It will press against the edges of your comfort. It will refuse to make you feel better if feeling better means going back to sleep.

If you allow it, it will pull you out of performance and into presence. It will confront the ways you've negotiated your power in exchange for being chosen. It will show you how to become the chooser.

What you'll find here is not a new identity to wear. It's a stripping away of everything you were told to be. And what's left when the pretending stops is something potent. Real. And unforgettable.

You've been conditioned to chase outcomes. The perfect relationship. The successful life. The dream version of yourself that is always one course, one manifestation, one reinvention away.

This book won't help you chase faster. It will help you stop chasing entirely. It will remind you that what you're seeking is not out there. It's not waiting at the end of a perfected morning routine or the next spiritual workshop. It's already in you. What's been missing isn't the next answer. What's been missing is permission.

Permission to stop performing. Permission to hold your standards. Permission to make people uncomfortable. Permission to let go of the parts of you that were only ever built to survive.

This book is a ritual of return. A path back to the woman who existed before the world told her what was acceptable.

You'll read things that feel like truth in your bones. You'll see parts of yourself reflected that you've long buried. You might feel called out. You might feel ignited. You might feel both.

Good.

You don't need another book that makes you feel good temporarily. You need one that pulls you deeper into your own knowing. One that awakens your edges, sharpens your voice, and makes you uncomfortable enough to finally stop playing small.

This isn't a workbook. It's an initiation. And every page is designed to do something to you — not just inform you, but shift you. You won't leave the same if you read with your whole self. That's not a threat. It's a promise.

You'll begin to notice the shift not in what you say, but in how you feel when you walk into a room. Not in how often you're praised, but in how rarely you second-guess yourself. The outer changes will come, but only because the inner ones will no longer wait.

You may start questioning relationships you've tolerated for too long. You may notice how often you've compromised your desires to keep the peace. You might see how deeply you've been conditioned to perform softness while hiding your power beneath layers of pleasing, apologizing, and hoping someone else would finally see you.

What this book offers isn't just permission. It's reflection. It's the voice that says, *You were right to feel uncomfortable with their expectations. You were right to want more. You were right to pull away when your soul knew something didn't fit, even if everyone else said it did.*

It gives language to what you've sensed all along. That your magnetism was never supposed to come from how agreeable you were. That your beauty isn't in how well you soften your presence, but in how fully you embody it. That your power isn't something to be feared or hidden — it's something to be remembered, reclaimed, and lived from.

This book will challenge your loyalty to outdated identities. The part of you that still thinks you must earn love by shape-shifting. The part that whispers, *Maybe if I just fix myself a little more, they'll stay.* It won't entertain those illusions. It will burn them. Because something more powerful wants to rise through you, and there's no room left for pretending.

You'll be asked to sit with discomfort. Not as punishment, but as transformation. You'll be asked to look at where you've abandoned yourself, where you've diluted your truth to avoid being too much, too emotional, too intense. And then, you'll be given the tools to stop doing that.

There is no fake empowerment here. No fluff. No recycled motivation wrapped in soft colors and empty promises. You will not be told to manifest your dream life while ignoring your nervous system, your trauma, or your suppressed rage. You'll be shown how to hold all of it — not perfectly, but powerfully.

If you came here looking for another way to be chosen, this book will disappoint you. But if you came here to choose yourself so fully that anything unaligned naturally falls away, you're exactly where you need to be. What this book will do for you is give you clarity. What it will do to you is disrupt the parts of you still addicted to being accepted more than being free.

It's not a guide to becoming someone new. It's a mirror showing you what you were before the world asked you to perform. It will not wrap you in false comfort. It will not hold your hand while you run back to safety. It will sit with you while you burn what no longer fits and remind you that fire is not destruction. It's purification.

And through that fire, you will emerge different. Not because this book gave you something you didn't have, but because it helped you remember what you were never meant to forget.

The woman who finishes this book is not the same woman who began it. She sees through games. She hears the voice of her own body louder than the noise outside of her. She no longer waits to be invited. She *knows* she belongs wherever she chooses to be.

What this book will give you is not instructions. It will give you your self. And once that happens, there's no going back.

Part I. The Reclamation

There comes a moment in every woman's life when something cracks. Not because she's broken, but because the shell she's been living in no longer fits. The masks grow heavy. The roles she once wore like armor start to suffocate. And beneath the surface, something ancient stirs — something too powerful, too wild, too real to stay buried any longer.

That moment is the beginning of reclamation.

This part of the journey isn't about adding more. It's not about fixing yourself or becoming someone better. It's about remembering who you were before the world told you who to be. It's about returning to the raw, unfiltered version of yourself — the one that existed before the conditioning, before the praise for politeness, before the silent agreements to keep the peace.

You were not born to be nice. You were born to be whole.

Reclamation is uncomfortable. It will ask you to look at everything you've inherited — from your mother, your culture, your relationships, your wounds — and ask, *Is this actually mine?* It will ask you to dig beneath your performative femininity and find the voice you silenced to make others feel safe. It will ask you to stop asking for permission and start listening to your own inner authority.

The reason this part matters is because everything else you'll build — your magnetism, your influence, your manifestation power — rests on the foundation of your truth. And you cannot live in your truth if you are still wrapped in stories that do not belong to you.

You can't reclaim power you're afraid to touch. You can't embody a self you've been trained to disown.

So this section will bring you face-to-face with the myths that have shaped you. It will take you into the shadow — not to get lost in it, but to find what was exiled there. Your anger. Your sensuality. Your chaos. Your voice. Your full, unedited self.

It will help you see how deeply the "good girl" script has cut into your life. How the demand for lightness has drained your depth. How your power has been made to feel unsafe not because it is dangerous, but because it cannot be controlled.

This is your undoing, in the best way. It's the unlearning of a thousand little rules that never belonged to your soul. And in their place, you'll begin to remember what it feels like to stand in your own energy without apology. To say no without explaining. To say yes without shame. To stop shrinking, negotiating, performing.

Reclamation is sacred work. It is gritty, beautiful, sometimes painful — and always worth it.

You are not too much. You are not too loud. You are not too wild, too emotional, too complicated. You are simply returning to yourself. And that return is magnetic.

Let the pages ahead be your permission. Let them be your mirror. Let them be the ignition that sparks your remembering.

It's time to stop playing roles.

It's time to come home to your power.

Welcome to Part I. Let the reclamation begin.

Chapter 1: The Masks You've Been Forced to Wear

The Silencing of the Wild Woman

There was a time when the feminine was not fragmented. When softness and strength, nurture and rage, grace and wildness lived in the same body without contradiction. The Wild Woman is not a fantasy. She is the original. She existed before the edits. Before the roles. Before the silence.

You've felt her. Not in theory, but in moments. In the instinct that told you to leave before your mind gave you permission. In the flush of desire that had no logic, only truth. In the fire that rose in your chest when you were disrespected and told to calm down.

The Wild Woman is not reckless. She is not dangerous in the way you were warned. She is simply uncontrollable. She listens to something deeper than rules — something older than politeness. And that makes her powerful in a way the world was never built to handle.

So they silenced her.

Not by force, but by shame. Not by chains, but by expectations so deeply woven into the fabric of society that you began to enforce them on yourself. You were taught to fear your wildness. To believe that instinct was impulsive, that sensuality was dangerous, that anger was unladylike, and that emotional truth was inconvenient. You were told to moderate, manage, tone it down. Be nice. Be sweet. Be quiet. Don't ruin the moment. Don't make it uncomfortable.

And slowly, you did.

Not because you were weak, but because you were wise. You learned to survive. You learned that dimming your light made others feel safe. You learned that hiding your intuition earned you praise. You learned that when you denied your wildness, you were more lovable, more desirable, more acceptable.

But deep down, something never stopped aching.

Because the Wild Woman doesn't die. She waits. She waits behind your people-pleasing. Behind your forced calm. Behind your polite smile in moments you want to scream. She waits in your hunger for more — more freedom, more fire, more truth, more life.

And she doesn't just want to be seen. She wants to be felt. Fully. Unapologetically. Completely.

This is where the tension lives. Between the version of you that's been shaped to keep the peace and the version that no longer wants to stay quiet just to be safe. Between the identity that earned approval and the one that threatens to unravel it.

The silencing didn't begin with you. It's generational. Woven into lineage. Passed from mother to daughter like an inheritance wrapped in good intentions. Be careful. Be quiet. Be good. Be grateful.

But just because it's been passed down doesn't mean you have to keep carrying it.

Reclaiming the Wild Woman begins by noticing the moments when you betray yourself. When you say yes with your mouth but no with your body. When you lower your voice even though your truth is rising. When you choose peace at the cost of your power.

These are not small moments. They are fractures. Every time you silence yourself, you split a little further from who you really are. And every time you speak, move, or choose from alignment, you begin to close that gap.

This is not about rebellion for the sake of noise. This is about realignment. This is about remembering that your wildness was never the problem. It was the compass you were taught to ignore.

Your wildness is not a flaw. It is not something to heal out of you or regulate into something more polite. It is not the thing that gets you into trouble. It is the part of you that *knows* when you're in the wrong room. It is the part of you that leaves when the red flags start waving. It is the voice that rises up in your chest when someone tries to cross a line you've already made clear.

You were taught to override her. To smile instead. To laugh it off. To make excuses for someone else's discomfort while abandoning your own truth. You were taught that being palatable was safer than being powerful. But the safety you were promised was conditional. It depended on you staying quiet, small, nice. It had nothing to do with being seen or respected. It had everything to do with being manageable.

What you may not realize yet is that this silencing didn't just cut you off from your voice. It cut you off from your magnetism. Because your power doesn't come from how likable you are. It comes from how embodied you are. And embodiment requires truth. Full truth. Not the edited, spiritualized version that makes everyone else feel comfortable.

It's in the rawness. The edge. The pulse of something that hasn't been filtered through politeness. You don't become magnetic by softening what's wild. You become magnetic by allowing it to live, breathe, and move through you. Not in chaos. In clarity. In certainty. In *presence*.

When the Wild Woman is silenced, the body keeps the score. You feel disconnected. Numb. Restless. Your voice gets shaky. Your boundaries get loose. You lose the sense that you are anchored in your own energy. That is the cost of silencing her. You might look composed, but inside you feel like you're disappearing.

And deep down, you know this isn't sustainable. You feel the pressure building. The edge getting sharper. The truth starting to rise in your throat no matter how much you try to hold it back. Because your Wild Woman doesn't disappear. She waits. She watches. And when you are finally ready, she rises.

She rises when you stop saying yes out of guilt. She rises when you allow yourself to be misunderstood rather than betray your own clarity. She rises when you choose your own peace over someone else's comfort. And when she rises, you begin to feel what real alignment tastes like.

You become unavailable for performance. You stop managing the emotions of others. You no longer apologize for your presence. You start leading with energy instead of explanation. That is the gift of your wildness. She makes you honest. She makes you powerful. She brings you back into your body and reminds you that your truth is not something to hide. It is something to honor.

This reclamation does not happen all at once. It happens in pieces. In the moment you say what you really mean. In the second you walk away instead of explaining yourself. In the quiet knowing that you don't have to justify your no. Every time you choose her, your nervous system recalibrates. Your self-respect solidifies. And your magnetism grows.

You were never meant to play a character. You were never meant to be praised for how well you disappear into expectations. You were meant to be felt. Fully. To walk into the world as the woman who trusts her body more than anyone's opinion. The woman who would rather be alone than perform. The woman who lives with the full range of her feminine expression — the wild, the wise, the soft, the sharp.

She is not missing. She is waiting.

And the moment you stop silencing her, everything changes.

How the Light-Only Narrative Disempowered You

You were told to stay in the light. To think positively. To be graceful. To forgive quickly. To raise your vibration, focus on the good, and not give energy to what feels heavy, sharp, or dark. On the surface, it sounded like healing. In practice, it often felt like erasure.

The obsession with light has become a cage dressed up as a cure. It's the kind of narrative that rewards compliance and silence, then calls it spiritual maturity. It tells you that your anger is low vibrational, that your sadness needs to be shifted, that your fear is a block to abundance. So you work harder to become more pleasant, more forgiving, more "high frequency," even when it means bypassing your truth.

This isn't healing. It's suppression.

The feminine was never meant to exist in fragments. She was never only radiant, only soft, only nurturing. She was never just the glow. She was also the fire. The shadow. The silence. The storm. To claim the light without integrating the dark is to live in half of your power while pretending it's the whole thing.

You may have been drawn to the light path because it felt safer. It offered order. Control. A sense that if you just thought the right thoughts, did the right rituals, meditated enough, or visualized the right future, you could bypass pain altogether. But you can't manifest your way out of what you haven't met within yourself. You can't rise if you're still afraid to fall.

The light-only narrative disempowers you because it separates you from your instinct. It tells you that discomfort is a sign of misalignment, rather than a doorway to truth. It labels the feminine fire as chaos instead of sacred disruption. It shames your emotional depth. It discourages necessary anger. It teaches you to spiritualize your own neglect.

How many times have you forgiven too fast because you thought holding onto anger would block your blessings? How often have you pushed down your truth to "keep your energy clean"? How much of your wildness have you muted because it didn't fit the softness others expected from a conscious woman?

This conditioning runs deep. And the hardest part is that it's often dressed in love. In softness. In community. You might have even found belonging in those spaces. But the cost was the parts of you that couldn't stay quiet just to be included. The parts of you that knew how to roar, how to rage, how to hold a boundary without smiling through it.

There's nothing wrong with the light. There is beauty in grace, compassion, and gentleness. But without the balance of the dark, light becomes performance. It becomes spiritual people-pleasing. It becomes a loop where you're constantly trying to "align" instead of allowing yourself to actually feel.

The feminine isn't here to be aligned at all times. She is cyclical. She births and destroys. She opens and withdraws. She invites and repels. The attempt to keep her locked in light is an attempt to domesticate what was never meant to be tamed.

If you've been living in the light-only model, you've probably felt the fatigue. The subtle shame when you're triggered. The pressure to get over things too quickly. The guilt when you feel envious, angry, or lost. That's not empowerment. That's spiritual discipline pretending to be freedom.

And deep down, you know it. You can feel the parts of you that have been waiting for permission to stop being so perfect and start being real.

The truth is, your power was never in how consistent your vibration was. It was never in how long you could stay smiling through discomfort. It was never in your ability to perform peace while swallowing truth. Your real power lives in your wholeness — in your ability to feel the full range of your feminine landscape without shame or fear.

There is intelligence in your anger. There is wisdom in your grief. There is transformation in your chaos. These are not signs that you are broken. They are signs that you are alive, that your body is speaking, that your energy is trying to lead you back to something real.

When you deny the dark, you deny yourself. And when you do that long enough, you begin to confuse suppression with strength. You wear emotional self-abandonment like a badge of spiritual honor. You become a master of appearing calm while silently eroding your own center.

This is why so many women who follow the light-only path feel drained, despite doing all the right things. They meditate. They journal. They visualize. And still, something feels off. Because you cannot elevate what you refuse to touch. You cannot heal what you're afraid to name. You cannot rise from a foundation that's built on the denial of your depth.

The feminine was never meant to be neat. She is not linear. She does not move in straight lines. She spirals. She bleeds. She breaks and rebuilds. Her evolution is messy, sacred, and unapologetic. And within that mess is where your real magnetism is born.

Magnetism is not manufactured in stillness. It's created in truth. It comes from being fully embodied in the moment you're in, not from bypassing it to reach something more palatable. It comes from honoring the part of you that feels wild, unsure, triggered, or tired — not from pretending those parts don't exist.

You were not made to glow all the time. You were made to burn, to rest, to rage, to rise. Your power is not in how well you keep the peace. Your power is in how deeply you live your truth — even when it disrupts expectations, even when it makes others uncomfortable, even when it scares you to be that honest with yourself.

This book does not ask you to abandon the light. It asks you to stop using it as a shield. It asks you to stop performing purity while your soul is calling for liberation. It asks you to come back to the parts of you that have been labeled too much, too dark, too emotional, too chaotic — and listen.

The feminine doesn't need fixing. She needs remembering. And part of that remembering includes the raw, unfiltered parts of your emotional reality. The parts that don't get reposted with aesthetic quotes. The parts that exist in your silence, your body, your unspoken knowing.

Those parts hold the keys.

You are not here to float above life. You are here to live it, to feel it, to embody it. Fully. Fiercely. Honestly.

That means allowing your light to shine without needing to dim your shadow. It means knowing that your radiance is real, but so is your rage. It means standing in your grace without being afraid of your edges.

This is the shift. Not to become a woman who only glows, but a woman who is grounded in the totality of her experience. A woman who knows that her emotional complexity is not a weakness, but a superpower. A woman who stops chasing alignment and starts embodying wholeness.

When you reclaim your full range, you stop being easy to manipulate. You stop being easy to mold. You stop being easy to dismiss. You become something rare. Something magnetic. Something unforgettable.

You become yourself. All of you. Not just the parts that earned praise, but the parts that refused to stay silent. And that is where your real freedom begins.

Recognizing the Cost of Being "Nice"

Being nice is praised in every part of your life. It's encouraged from the moment you're able to speak. Say thank you. Don't interrupt. Smile. Be polite. Be patient. Be understanding. These instructions come early and often. And over time, they become part of your identity. You learn that being nice isn't just good — it's expected.

But what no one tells you is the cost.

Nice is not the same as kind. Kindness is a conscious choice. It comes from strength, from self-awareness, from alignment. Niceness, the kind that's conditioned into women, is something else entirely. It's performance. It's appeasement. It's a way to make yourself acceptable in a world that rewards your silence more than your truth.

You've been taught to be nice even when someone crosses your boundaries. To smile through discomfort. To forgive before you're ready. To take responsibility for emotions that don't belong to you. To soften your reactions so others won't feel confronted. And somewhere along the way, being nice stops being a choice. It becomes a default — a reflex that activates any time your nervous system senses conflict, rejection, or disapproval.

This is where the damage begins.

Because when you're nice at the expense of being real, you slowly start to disappear. You agree when you want to say no. You listen when you want to walk away. You make space for others while shrinking your own presence. And then you wonder why you feel unseen, unappreciated, or resentful.

The world tells you that being nice makes you good. But what it really makes you is accessible. Contained. Easy to handle. You become the woman who doesn't ask for too much, doesn't make things difficult, doesn't disturb the peace. You become the emotional buffer in rooms where people refuse to grow. You become the one who understands, who absorbs, who explains — even when you're the one being mistreated.

And the worst part? You're praised for it.

You're told you're mature. That you're gracious. That you're compassionate. And those words feel like approval, but they're often just rewards for how well you've managed to abandon yourself without making a scene.

28

This pattern doesn't just show up in your relationships with others. It starts to shape your relationship with yourself. You begin to second-guess your instincts. You hesitate before speaking your truth. You worry more about how you're being perceived than whether you're being honest. And over time, you forget what it feels like to choose yourself without guilt.

The cost of being nice is not just emotional. It's energetic. You drain yourself by holding space that was never yours to hold. You stretch beyond your capacity. You tolerate too much. And each time you do, you train your nervous system to associate self-abandonment with safety.

This is not who you were born to be.

You weren't created to be a peacekeeper for people who can't handle your truth. You weren't designed to carry the weight of everyone's emotions while ignoring your own. You weren't meant to live your life in emotional compromise.

Being nice might keep the surface calm, but underneath, it creates a storm of resentment, depletion, and quiet rage. And that storm is trying to tell you something.

It's not asking you to become cruel or harsh. It's asking you to become honest. With yourself. With others. With the part of you that's tired of packaging your truth in politeness just to stay likable.

You can't be fully expressed and perpetually agreeable. You can't hold your power and keep everyone comfortable. You can't be deeply respected while constantly self-editing.

You weren't made to be liked by everyone. You were made to be known by yourself. And that knowing requires truth, not performance. You cannot be fully in your feminine power while constantly bending to please others. That power requires your full presence, your full voice, your full alignment — even when it makes someone else uncomfortable, even when it breaks the image they've created of you.

Niceness often becomes a shield. You use it to protect yourself from rejection, from conflict, from being called difficult. But a shield that keeps others from disapproving of you also keeps you from living in your integrity. It filters everything you say through the question, "How will they take this?" instead of, "Is this what I really mean?"

The more you perform niceness, the more disconnected you become from your instincts. You feel something in your body, but you override it. You

29

know something is off, but you smile through it. You want to say no, but your mouth says yes because it feels safer in the moment.

This disconnect becomes dangerous, not just emotionally, but energetically. Because every time you betray yourself in small ways, you start to believe you can't trust your own truth. You start looking to others to confirm what's right for you. You lose your inner compass. And without that compass, you become vulnerable to manipulation, confusion, and energetic fragmentation.

There's a reason why "nice girls" often feel the most drained, the most resentful, the most unseen. It's not because they're weak. It's because they've built an entire identity around being what others need — while quietly starving the parts of themselves that crave boldness, directness, and sovereignty.

You don't owe anyone constant access to your softness. You don't have to smile to keep a conversation light when you'd rather walk away. You don't have to keep being the one who understands everyone else's pain while yours goes unspoken.

The cost of being nice is your wholeness. And the longer you stay in that role, the more distant your real self becomes. You start forgetting what it feels like to say something without rehearsing it first. To take up space without shrinking. To be direct without feeling guilty. To protect your energy without explaining yourself.

Reclaiming yourself doesn't mean becoming rude or reactive. It means becoming honest. It means recognizing that the version of you who always says yes, who always accommodates, who always makes others feel safe even at her own expense — that version is not the most loving or empowered part of you. She is the part that learned to survive. But she is not the part that will lead you into your power.

Your feminine magnetism does not live in politeness. It lives in presence. In truth. In the energy that says, *I am here, and I do not need to twist myself to belong.* That kind of presence cannot be faked. It doesn't come from saying the right things. It comes from being in full integrity with what you feel, what you want, and what you are no longer willing to tolerate.

Let go of the idea that you must be liked to be safe. You are not here to be the easiest woman in the room. You are here to be the most rooted, the most real, the most magnetic version of yourself — and that version does not chase approval. She does not explain away her boundaries. She does not confuse silence with peace.

She speaks. She stands firm. She lets her "no" carry weight and her presence carry meaning.

The world may not praise her the way it praised your niceness. But your body will thank you. Your energy will thank you. Your life will shift in ways it never could while you were still trapped in the habit of being digestible.

This is your invitation to stop shrinking under the weight of being nice and start expanding into the truth of being powerful. Not for attention. Not for validation. But because you finally remember what it feels like to be fully, unapologetically you.

Chapter 2: Shadow Work as a Feminine Ritual

What the Shadow Really Is (and Isn't)

You've heard the word everywhere. Shadow work. Shadow integration. Embracing your shadow. But for most women, the shadow remains more concept than lived experience. It gets talked about in whispers or turned into aesthetic language. And while the idea is everywhere, the truth of it remains elusive.

The shadow isn't evil. It's not your darkness in the way the world has defined darkness. It's not sin, shame, or wrongness. It's not something to fix. And it's definitely not something to get rid of.

The shadow is any part of you that you've learned to suppress in order to be accepted.

That's it. It's not mysterious. It's not dramatic. It's the parts of you that went underground the moment you realized they made others uncomfortable. It's your anger if you were raised to be quiet. It's your sensuality if you were told your body was dangerous. It's your ambition if you were taught to be humble and accommodating. It's your need for attention if you were praised for being selfless.

The shadow forms early. It's not born from your flaws, but from your brilliance — the brilliance that made others feel something they didn't know how to hold. So you learned to hide it. And in that hiding, you internalized the belief that those parts of you were bad. Too much. Shameful. Unsafe.

The irony is that the shadow doesn't stop influencing you just because you've buried it. In fact, the more you deny it, the more power it has. It starts to express itself in sideways ways. You snap at the wrong people. You sabotage relationships that are too good. You overwork, over-give, over-explain. You project. You shrink. You overcompensate with performance and perfection, not realizing that what you're trying to prove is rooted in what you're afraid to admit.

When left unseen, the shadow runs your life from behind the scenes. But when brought into awareness, it becomes one of your greatest sources of power.

Most people avoid shadow work because they think it's about facing their worst traits. But the truth is, shadow work is just as often about reclaiming your beauty as it is about facing your pain. Because your shadow holds not just the things you were shamed for, but also the things you weren't allowed to celebrate. Your boldness. Your confidence. Your desire to be seen. Your ability to take up space.

You didn't just hide your wounds. You hid your brilliance, too.

And this is where it becomes essential for the dark feminine path. Because as long as those parts remain buried, you will continue to live a life shaped by who the world trained you to be — not by who you truly are. You'll keep adjusting yourself to stay safe. You'll keep attracting situations that reflect your unacknowledged pain. You'll keep seeking validation for a version of you that was never whole to begin with.

The shadow is not your enemy. It's your invitation. It's the gateway back to everything you've silenced. It's the place where your voice got stuck, where your energy froze, where your real expression went quiet.

Facing it doesn't make you less feminine. It makes you *real*. It brings your wholeness back into the light — not to clean it up, but to integrate it.

You are not here to be perfect. You are here to be whole.

You've spent years trying to elevate yourself by rejecting your shadow. You've labeled discomfort as misalignment. You've tried to meditate away the mess. You've told yourself that being positive is the answer, while secretly feeling the weight of all the things you're not allowed to feel. The truth is, you've been trying to build your power on a fractured foundation. And deep down, you know it hasn't been working.

Your shadow isn't waiting to be healed. It's waiting to be *seen*. That's the starting point. You don't need to fix it. You need to sit with it. Feel what it's been carrying. Name what you've never had the space to say out loud. Because everything you suppress gains strength in silence. But once it's brought into awareness, it stops running your life from the shadows.

This is not easy work. It will bring you face to face with the stories you've been told about who you're allowed to be. It will reveal how much of your identity is built on adaptation. It will show you how often you've sacrificed authenticity for acceptance, how often you've betrayed yourself in small ways to avoid confrontation or rejection. But what you gain is priceless.

You gain clarity. The kind that doesn't come from outside affirmation, but from internal alignment. You start recognizing patterns not as flaws, but as signals. You stop making yourself wrong for having edges, depth, or complexity. You stop trying to be light all the time and start becoming *real* all the time.

That shift changes everything.

You begin to hold yourself differently. You stop overexplaining. You speak without softening every truth to make others comfortable. You feel your emotions as they come, without making them mean something about your worth. You stop trying to be likable and start becoming magnetic.

There is something unshakable about a woman who has met her shadow. Not because she is polished, but because she is *honest*. She no longer fears her own depth. She no longer hides when things feel messy. She doesn't need to control every perception because she is not fragmented inside. She has made peace with the parts of herself that once felt dangerous.

And in doing so, she becomes whole.

This is the invitation shadow work extends to you. To stop performing. To stop fixing. To stop running toward perfection and instead come back to presence. Not for the sake of healing as a project, but for the sake of coming home to who you were before you learned to hide.

You don't need to be fearless. You need to be willing. Willing to turn toward the discomfort instead of away. Willing to ask, "What part of me am I avoiding right now?" Willing to see the shadow not as a threat, but as a teacher.

Some of the most magnetic women you'll ever meet are not the most healed. They are the most *integrated*. They are the ones who have looked themselves in the eye without flinching. The ones who have cried over the versions of themselves they had to let go of, not because they were unworthy, but because they were incomplete. They are women who walk into the world unmasked. And that energy — that raw, unfiltered presence — is unforgettable.

You are not meant to live at war with yourself. You are not meant to silence your depth just to be understood. You are not meant to outgrow your shadow. You are meant to walk with it. You are meant to see it, speak to it, learn from it.

The shadow is not the end of your light. It's the beginning of your embodiment. When you embrace it, you stop hiding. And when you stop hiding, you become free. Fully. Finally. And on your terms.

Turning Pain into Power: Shadow Integration 101

There's a point on the path when you realize pain isn't the enemy. It's not the thing to avoid, bypass, or bury beneath affirmations. It's the entry point. The portal. The place where your soul starts speaking in a language louder than your performance can cover. And if you listen, if you allow yourself to go there without judgment, that pain becomes the very thing that sets you free.

Shadow integration begins where avoidance ends.

This work is not about wallowing. It's not about sitting in your wounds and calling it growth. It's about meeting what you've been trained to suppress and allowing it to *move*. Not to perform healing. Not to impress anyone with your awareness. But to reclaim the parts of you that got frozen in time when your body decided it wasn't safe to be fully seen.

Most women carry emotional weight they don't even realize they're still holding. Old betrayals that haven't been grieved. Childhood moments where their bigness was punished. Silences that taught them speaking up was dangerous. That pain gets buried in the body. It doesn't disappear. It simply waits. And over time, it becomes tension. It becomes emotional reactivity. It becomes energetic confusion. And it silently shapes every relationship you have — including the one with yourself.

Shadow integration is the process of giving voice to those silent places. It's the courageous act of turning toward the discomfort rather than decorating it with spiritual language. And it starts with a question most people are too afraid to ask:

What have I not let myself feel?

Most of the pain you carry is not just about what happened. It's about the story you created around it. The shame. The self-blame. The belief that your pain made you weak, dramatic, unlovable, or broken. That story is what creates the wound, not the pain itself. The story is what keeps it alive long after the moment has passed.

When you approach your shadow from a place of curiosity instead of judgment, everything changes. You stop labeling yourself. You stop trying to force clarity. You begin to feel your way into truth. And that truth doesn't always come with immediate answers. Sometimes it comes with tears. With trembling. With a deep exhale that says, *Finally. I don't have to carry this alone.*

There is nothing linear about shadow work. It's not something you check off a list. It's not a one-time journaling session or a trendy ritual. It's a lifelong relationship with your own inner landscape — one that demands honesty, patience, and the willingness to sit with what is unresolved without trying to fix it too quickly.

This is where many people get stuck. They want transformation to look clean. They want to move through their shadow without having to feel the fire. But integration is not sterile. It's messy. It's emotional. It brings you face to face with the places where you still don't trust yourself. And that confrontation is where the real power lives.

Because when you stop running, your pain starts to teach you. It teaches you where you've abandoned yourself. Where you've made yourself small to survive. Where you've performed safety at the expense of your truth. And in that teaching, it gives you the exact material you need to step into your power.

The pain becomes a map. Not a burden, but a guide. And as you trace it back, as you follow the feelings you once feared, you begin to find pieces of yourself that you thought were lost forever.

You don't retrieve those parts of yourself by forcing them to behave. You retrieve them by witnessing them. By meeting the version of you that was silenced, shamed, or dismissed and saying, *I see you. I hear you. You didn't deserve to be erased.* That kind of presence heals more than any technique ever could. Your shadow is not asking for perfection. It's asking for honesty. For space. For your willingness to let go of who you think you need to be in order to feel worthy. And once you give it that space, you stop needing to protect yourself with constant control. You stop clinging to emotional armor that no longer fits. You start living from a place of grounded truth rather than surface-level harmony.

This is the alchemy. The place where pain begins to transmute into power. Not by changing what happened, but by changing your relationship to it. You no longer see your pain as something that weakened you. You start to see it as the forge. The moment you were carved open enough to discover what was real beneath the performance. That depth becomes your power.

When your shadow is integrated, you become emotionally honest. You don't pretend to be okay when you're not. You don't smile through boundaries being crossed. You don't use spiritual phrases to mask emotional avoidance. You learn to be with what is, without turning it into a story about your worth.

You stop needing everyone to understand you because you no longer misunderstand yourself. That clarity radiates. It changes how you walk, how you speak, how you love. It gives you access to your feminine energy in its full spectrum — the part that nurtures and the part that protects. The part that feels deeply and the part that draws firm lines.

This is what shadow integration *does*. It doesn't erase the past. It returns your power to you in the present. The power to choose a different response. The power to no longer abandon yourself in familiar ways. The power to feel without being consumed and to express without shrinking.

Pain that is not integrated becomes a pattern. It repeats itself in relationships, in self-talk, in your nervous system's responses to life. But pain that is felt, understood, and integrated becomes wisdom. It becomes a steady presence inside you. A reminder that you can hold yourself through anything, not because you are detached, but because you are connected to every part of yourself.

This is not about becoming invincible. It's about becoming whole. When you are whole, you stop fearing your edges. You stop fearing discomfort. You stop fearing your own intensity. And when you stop fearing those things, you become someone who is very difficult to manipulate.

You are no longer pulled into power dynamics that drain you. You are no longer waiting for others to validate your experience. You become the woman who listens to herself first. Who trusts what she feels. Who acts on her knowing. And that is what makes you magnetic.

People will feel the difference. They won't always be able to explain it. But they will feel it. They will feel that you are not chasing anything. That you are not pretending. That you are not performing. You are *being*. Fully. And that kind of presence is rare.

Shadow integration is not a one-time ritual. It is a return. Again and again. A remembering. A recalibration. And with each return, you become more of yourself. Not a version you created to survive, but the version that was always there underneath the layers.

This is the path of the dark feminine. Not lightwashed, not bypassed, not controlled. Fully felt. Fully known. Fully embodied. This is where pain becomes power. This is where you stop hiding. And this is where your true life begins.

Rituals to Transmute Shame, Guilt, and Suppressed Desire

Shame is one of the most powerful silencers of feminine energy. It doesn't just close your throat. It closes your body. It makes you doubt your instincts, question your desires, and apologize for wanting anything that doesn't fit the script you were handed.

Guilt often follows close behind. Not the healthy kind that signals when you've crossed a boundary of your own integrity, but the inherited kind. The kind passed down through generations of women taught to feel bad for needing too much, expressing too much, taking up too much space. The kind that trains you to apologize before you speak, and to shrink even when you're starving to expand.

And then there's desire. The part of you that still pulses under the layers. The part you try to manage with logic, hide behind productivity, or suppress under roles. Desire that is too raw, too wild, too much for the world you were raised in. It doesn't go away. It waits.

These energies — shame, guilt, and suppressed desire — are not just emotional. They are stored in the body. In the hips, in the chest, in the voice. They create tension, fatigue, disconnection. You don't just feel blocked. You feel cut off from your own life force.

That's where ritual comes in.

Ritual is not about being dramatic or mystical for the sake of appearance. It's about creating intentional space to meet these energies in a new way. Not to reject or bypass them, but to transmute them. To shift their frequency by giving them what they've always needed — presence, expression, and permission.

You don't need complex tools to do this. You need willingness. You need a private moment of truth. A place where you're no longer performing. Where you can let the shame rise without analyzing it. Where you can speak the guilt out loud without trying to justify it. Where you can feel your desire without censoring or moralizing it.

A ritual is a container. A space that says, *This is safe. This is sacred. This gets to exist.* In that space, the emotion is no longer something to hide from. It becomes material you can work with. You become the alchemist, not the victim of emotional weight you were never taught how to hold.

There is no one way to do this. But what matters is that it's embodied. This work can't live only in your head. It has to pass through your body. That's where the energy lives. That's where it gets stored. That's where it's released. A ritual to transmute shame might begin with naming it. Out loud. No softening, no filtering. Saying the thing you've never said. The memory. The secret. The belief that still haunts you. You speak it not to relive it, but to unfreeze it. The moment it's voiced, it moves. It stops festering in silence and starts transforming through sound, through breath, through expression. A ritual to release guilt might begin with asking whose guilt you're really carrying. Your own? Or the guilt you absorbed from others who couldn't handle your autonomy, your pleasure, your truth? You might write it out. You might burn the paper. You might dance it out, sob it out, shake it loose. The release must be physical. You are not just releasing thoughts. You are releasing the charge they left behind.

Desire asks for something different. It doesn't want to be released. It wants to be reclaimed.

Desire doesn't need to be healed. It needs to be heard. It needs to be witnessed without judgment, without analysis, without the immediate impulse to control it or turn it into something useful. Your desire doesn't need to be productive. It doesn't need to be pure. It doesn't need to be justified through spiritual logic or moral frameworks. It just wants to be felt. When desire is suppressed for too long, it doesn't disappear. It distorts. It shows up as restlessness, anxiety, compulsive behavior, or emotional numbness. It creates a silent hunger that's hard to name but impossible to ignore. You might find yourself overworking, overthinking, overgiving — all while feeling strangely disconnected from your own body. This is the cost of exile. And the way back is embodiment.

One of the most potent rituals you can offer yourself is to *sit with your desire without trying to edit it*. Light a candle. Close your eyes. Let your body lead the experience. Ask yourself, *What do I want that I've never let myself admit?* Stay there. Let the images come. Let the sensations move through you. If your throat tightens, breathe deeper. If you feel heat rise in your chest or between your hips, don't flinch. Let it unfold.

There is power in naming. There is power in wanting without shrinking. There is power in holding space for your own fire without needing to perform it for someone else's approval. That's what reclamation looks like.

Not becoming someone new, but peeling back everything that told you your hunger was too much.

The body holds memory. It remembers the moments you were told to quiet down, cover up, act appropriate, think of others, be modest, be good. These instructions didn't just train your behavior. They trained your nervous system. That's why desire can feel threatening. It represents the self you had to lock away to stay safe. But you are not that girl anymore. You are the woman who gets to choose. And choice starts with awareness.

A ritual can be simple. A mirror. A private space. Your voice. Your breath. Your hands on your own skin. It doesn't need to look a certain way. It needs to feel honest. You are not performing. You are remembering. This is not about seduction. It's about sovereignty.

Guilt may try to creep in, especially when desire starts to surface after years of being hidden. It may whisper that you're selfish, reckless, inappropriate, unspiritual. Let the voice come. Let it speak. And then ask, *Whose voice is this really?* That voice was inherited. It is not your truth. It was designed to keep you obedient, not fulfilled.

Your feminine energy is not a passive glow. It is primal. It is untamed. It is the force of creation itself. And it cannot be fully accessed while carrying the weight of shame and guilt that never belonged to you. The rituals you create are not just for healing. They are for awakening. They are for remembering that your body is not something to tolerate. It is something to inhabit fully.

When shame dissolves, your voice becomes clearer. When guilt is released, your boundaries become firmer. When desire is reclaimed, your magnetism becomes undeniable. These shifts are not dramatic. They are sacred. They happen in the quiet spaces where you choose to show up for yourself without needing permission or praise.

Transmutation is not always loud. Sometimes it looks like a woman sitting in her truth for the first time in years. Sometimes it looks like movement without choreography. Sometimes it sounds like silence after a scream that was never allowed to be heard.

These rituals are yours to define. They do not belong to a lineage, a method, or a system. They belong to your body, your knowing, your experience. Let them evolve. Let them be messy. Let them feel like home.

Because what you're really doing is not just releasing shame or guilt. You are restoring access to your power. And once that access is open, it becomes very hard to ever go back to pretending you are not whole.

Chapter 3: Reclaiming the Archetypes

The Dark Goddess: Lilith, Kali, Medusa & the Others Who Were Banished

There's a reason the names Lilith, Kali, and Medusa evoke a certain tension in the body. A flicker of intrigue. A shadow of discomfort. A magnetic pull wrapped in centuries of warning. These names weren't meant to be repeated with reverence. They were meant to be whispered in fear, kept outside the circle of sanctified femininity. Not because they were evil — but because they refused to be tamed.

The Dark Goddess is not one woman, one archetype, or one myth. She is the embodiment of everything that has been cast out of the acceptable feminine. Rage, wildness, erotic power, destruction, death, creation without permission. She is the mother you were told to fear. The voice you were told to silence. The energy you were trained to disown.

And yet, she lives in you.

Let's start with Lilith — often painted as a demon, the original rebel, the first wife of Adam who refused to submit. She is one of the earliest symbols of a woman who walked away from control, even when the price was exile. She did not choose to be second. She did not agree to be remade in anyone's image but her own. For that, she was written out of the story and demonized for eternity. But Lilith was never evil. She was sovereign. She was sexual. She was free. And that made her dangerous.

Her exile is not a myth limited to the past. It's a mirror. How many times have you walked away from something because it required you to shrink? How many times have you been punished, judged, or labeled just for choosing yourself? That is the Lilith in you. She doesn't beg. She doesn't obey. She doesn't explain. She reminds you that you were never meant to be someone's version of good.

Then there is Kali — fierce, blood-soaked, tongue out, dancing over the body of her consort. She is destruction and rebirth in one breath. Western narratives often try to soften her or misread her entirely. But Kali is not here to be pretty or polite. She is the destroyer of illusions, the sword that severs

44

ego, the mother who burns everything that isn't real. She is chaos as a sacred force. And that chaos is not random. It is cleansing.

To work with the energy of Kali is to allow part of yourself to die. The part that clings. The part that lies. The part that would rather numb than feel. Kali does not whisper affirmations. She breaks you open. And in doing so, she gives birth to something far more honest. She represents the truth that sometimes things must fall apart before they can be real.

Medusa, another banished feminine figure, holds a different kind of power. Her story was twisted into a warning: look at her, and you'll turn to stone. She was made into a monster, but that's not how her myth began. Medusa was once a mortal woman, violated in a temple, punished for being a victim, and transformed into a creature of terror. But there's something deeper in her story — a woman who, after being stripped of power, was given the ability to petrify with a single glance. She no longer had to fight. She only had to be seen.

What if Medusa isn't a monster at all, but a symbol of the woman whose trauma became her armor? What if the snakes weren't punishment, but protection? What if the ones who turned to stone were those who could no longer look at her and see only weakness?

The Dark Goddess doesn't just belong to myth. She belongs to every woman who has ever been told she was too much. Every woman who has been punished for her anger, feared for her sexuality, erased for her power. *And yet, she rises.*

She rises in your boundaries. In the moment you say no without softening it. In the night you choose solitude over performance. In the kiss you give with your whole soul, not as a transaction but as a transmission. She rises in your silence that doesn't need to justify. In your anger that isn't chaotic but clean. In your longing that burns without shame.

You don't need to worship these archetypes. You need to recognize them as living currents in your blood. To see how their exile mirrors your own. They were not banished because they failed as feminine beings. They were banished because they refused to sever themselves to fit a system that only allowed women to exist as saints, mothers, or martyrs. The truth is, the women who carry the energy of the Dark Goddess are not rare. What's rare is the world that allows them to remain whole.

There is Eris, the goddess of strife and discord, who threw the golden apple that led to a war. She was left out of a wedding feast because her presence was too inconvenient. But Eris did not destroy peace. She exposed the illusion of it. She revealed the fault lines already there. Her chaos was not random. It was honest. It surfaced the truth that had been politely buried under diplomacy. This is the power of the woman who stops trying to keep everything smooth. Who lets the rupture speak. Who sees the cost of harmony built on suppression.

There is Hecate, the keeper of crossroads and thresholds. She was never malevolent, but she moved in liminal spaces, guiding the dead, holding the lantern in the dark. Her wisdom was in the shadows. Not as a trap, but as a bridge. She reminds you that power isn't just found in light and clarity. Sometimes it's in what cannot be named yet. In the pause between decisions. In the quiet knowing that doesn't rush.

Each of these figures carries a forgotten permission. A key to an inner gate that may have been locked long ago. Not to be worshipped from a distance, but to be integrated as part of your own living myth. Their stories were distorted so that you would fear them. But what you were taught to fear was the raw, undiluted version of you.

This chapter of your reclamation is not about becoming them. It's about remembering you were never separate.

When you feel rage rise and don't collapse into guilt, Lilith is present. When you walk away from a dynamic that once defined your worth, Hecate is walking with you. When you face your pain and let it purify rather than shame you, Kali is watching. When your gaze says, "I see everything and still I do not flinch," Medusa speaks through you.

To embody the Dark Goddess is to be unbothered by palatability. To let your erotic energy be sacred and sovereign. To stop translating your fire into something softer just so others can stay comfortable. There is a quiet revolution in the woman who no longer fears being too much. She is not reckless. She is precise. She knows when to wield silence and when to use her voice like a blade.

The return of these archetypes is not a trend. It is a necessity. Their presence is an antidote to generations of spiritual gaslighting, where love was taught as obedience and power was masked as purity. You are not here to perform feminine light. You are here to embody feminine wholeness. That includes the shadows. That includes the flame. That includes the part of you that was never broken, just buried under layers of social obedience.

The Dark Goddess doesn't need to be reclaimed. She needs to be re-invited into your inner temple, not as a threat, but as the guardian of your most untamed truth.

She was never the villain.

She was always the key.

Creating Your Personal Dark Feminine Archetype

You are not here to simply inherit archetypes. You are here to *become* one.
The goddesses, wild women, and dark feminine forces we've explored are not meant to be copied. They are mirrors. Catalysts. Reminders of what already lives inside you. Their power is not in their mythology, but in their ability to awaken your own. That awakening is the first step, but embodiment is the real initiation.

You've met Lilith, Kali, Medusa. You've felt their fire, their refusal, their reclamation. Now it's time to craft your own. Because your life has not followed their exact script. Your scars have a different shape. Your desires speak in a different tongue. Your shadow carries different codes. You are not here to fit into someone else's myth. You are here to write your own.

To create your personal archetype is to name the unnamable in you. The part that has never bowed. The part that survived the silencing, the distortion, the fear. The one who never left, even when the rest of you forgot she existed.

She is not a fantasy version of you. She is the most distilled, raw, unapologetic frequency of your truth.

You do not need her to be liked. You need her to be whole.

This archetype is not a costume. She is not performance. She is the convergence of your rage, your grace, your wounds, your power, your tenderness, and your untouchable essence. She is the energy that walks beside you when your voice shakes but you speak anyway. When you say no without smiling. When you leave the room and take your radiance with you. This process is not about inventing. It is about remembering.

There is a part of you that already knows what she looks like. How she moves. What she would never tolerate again. The way she seduces reality. The way she knows exactly who she is, even when others project everything they want her to be. She does not negotiate her value. She does not explain her intuition. She is not available for the games of those who need her small to feel powerful.

She is not bound by rules that were never made for her kind. She doesn't burn herself to make others warm. She doesn't apologize for wanting deeply. She lets the world adjust to her frequency.

You might meet her in dreams. In moments of intensity when you act before thinking and feel more alive than ever. In the way your body tightens when you betray yourself. In the clarity that cuts through you when you're about to choose comfort over truth. She's there. She's always been there. You've just been told she was too much to let live.

Now, she becomes the blueprint. The internal reference point. The one you return to when you're about to fall into old patterns. She is the version of you that holds the line. Who doesn't flinch. Who doesn't shrink. And yet, she is not hard. She is not closed. She is not disconnected. Her softness is earned. Her surrender is sacred. Her power is never on loan.

This is where the work becomes personal. Visceral. Unmistakable. We are no longer studying the archetype. You are becoming her.

To step into her requires discernment. You will have to unhook from the performance of power. You will have to recognize the ways you've confused rebellion with freedom, attention with magnetism, control with influence. She will not let you posture. She will not let you cling to the illusions that once gave you a false sense of safety. She strips away the noise until only the real remains.

There is no formula. No template. This is a descent into yourself. A listening. A sculpting. Some will find her in silence. Others through movement. Some through art, or rage, or ritual. She may arrive through erotic dreams, flashes of memory, or sudden surges of knowing that seem to come from somewhere ancient. Let her speak. Let her show you how she wants to move through you. Do not demand that she be logical. She will never fit into linear understanding.

She is multi-tonal. She is contradiction. She is shadow and light braided together with unapologetic elegance. You may feel tempted to polish her, to make her more palatable. Don't. She does not need refining. She needs reverence. She does not need to be digestible. She needs to be respected. This is not the version of you designed to make others comfortable. This is the version that makes the earth shift under your feet because she knows she belongs.

You may fear her at first. You may worry what others will think when she takes the lead. But when she walks into a room, she brings your whole self with her. She is the keeper of your boundaries, the protector of your deepest truth, the one who says "enough" and means it. She is not here to destroy you. She is here to rebuild you on foundations that cannot be shaken by projection, rejection, or betrayal.

You don't have to explain her to anyone. You don't need others to see her, validate her, or understand her. She is for you. And when you live from her, the right people will feel it. They'll sense the electricity in your presence, the clarity in your silence, the self-possession in your gaze. This energy cannot be imitated. It cannot be faked. It can only be remembered, reclaimed, and embodied.

This is not a mask. This is a homecoming.

Let her have a name if it helps you speak to her. Let her have a voice if it helps you hear her clearly. Let her be adorned or stripped bare, wild or composed, loud or whispering. She will shift as you shift. She will evolve as you evolve. But her essence remains the same. She is the frequency of your power when it is no longer filtered through fear.

You don't need to force her out. She is waiting for your permission. Not the timid kind. The kind that is felt deep in your bones, when you finally decide that you will no longer live in fragments. That you will not keep her locked behind the conditioning of being "nice," "safe," or "desirable" in someone else's terms.

You are not too much. You are not broken. You are not intimidating. You are remembering who you were before you forgot.

This archetype you are shaping is not an escape from yourself. She is the part of you that could never be erased. She is your clarity in chaos, your power in vulnerability, your voice when you've been told to be quiet. She is the edge you were taught to file down. Now, she becomes your blade. Not to harm, but to cut through the illusions that have kept you small.

And once you meet her, truly meet her, you won't be able to unsee her. You won't want to.

Because she is you.

Unedited. Unashamed. Undeniable.

Channeling Myth Into Modern Magnetic Identity

There's a reason myths have survived for thousands of years. They carry truths too powerful, too raw, too wild to be flattened by time. Myths are not just stories. They are blueprints. Encoded in every goddess, monster, oracle, and seductress is a mirror for your own becoming. You don't have to "believe" in mythology to be shaped by it. It's already in your bones, waiting to be activated.

This is not about pretending to be someone you're not. It's about recognizing the archetypal forces that have always lived inside you and letting them speak through your style, your voice, your posture, your presence. The mythic self isn't fantasy. It's the version of you that moves through the world with depth, resonance, and unapologetic clarity. She isn't trying to be liked. She isn't seeking approval. She's aligned with something older and far more compelling than validation. She's magnetic because she's mythic.

When you begin to channel myth into your modern identity, you stop performing and start embodying. You move from mimicry into mastery. You are no longer outsourcing your confidence to fleeting trends or social approval. You're rooted in something elemental, something that cannot be taken from you. You don't need to shout to be heard. You carry the echo of centuries in your gaze. You don't need to chase to be chosen. You become the one who chooses.

Think of the women in ancient stories who refused to shrink. Lilith who would not submit. Persephone who moved between worlds. Kali who danced in destruction to birth a new order. Medusa whose gaze turned those who sought to violate her into stone. These were not passive figures. They were not waiting to be saved. They were thresholds. They were initiations. They were symbols of what a woman becomes when she reclaims what has been denied.

Your modern identity doesn't need to look like them in costume. That's not the point. It's not about aesthetics. It's about energy. It's about deciding that you will no longer dilute yourself to be digestible. That you will dress, speak, and move in ways that express who you truly are beneath the filters and the masks. You can be soft and still carry the weight of thunder. You can be elegant and still be dangerous. The archetypal feminine contains every contradiction.

51

This kind of identity doesn't beg for attention. It bends attention around it. When you walk into a room, your presence carries a frequency that speaks before you open your mouth. People may not even understand why they feel drawn to you, why their eyes keep returning to you, why your words linger in their mind. But it's not about being loud or flashy. It's about being clear. Clear in your values, in your energy, in your posture, in your being.

The mythic doesn't belong to the past. It belongs to the woman who dares to remember her power in the present. She knows that she doesn't need to erase her edges to be worthy. She doesn't need to suppress her sensuality to be taken seriously. She doesn't need to trade mystery for relatability. She simply needs to walk with the awareness that every movement, every glance, every choice is a thread in the myth she is weaving.

And that myth? It doesn't have to follow anyone else's structure. It doesn't need a linear plot or a neat ending. It can spiral, expand, contract, rupture, and rebuild. Just like you. That's the power of archetypal living. You become a symbol in motion — not to be idolized, but to be lived. You become the myth that others feel before they can name it.

When you begin to live this way, you don't just change how others see you. You change how you see yourself. Your reflection stops being a surface-level check for flaws. It becomes a reminder. A portal. You start to dress not for trends, but as an act of ritual. You choose words not to impress, but to pierce. You stop wasting energy trying to be understood by those who have no capacity to meet you in your depth. You stop contorting to fit rooms that were never designed to hold the fullness of you.

This is not about performance. It's about frequency. The mythic woman doesn't chase visibility. She becomes inevitable. Her presence is not always loud, but it is unmistakable. Her stillness carries more command than someone else's noise. Her silence is not submission. It is sovereignty. She doesn't wait for permission to express herself. She expresses because it is who she is. Not for effect. Not for applause. But because she has remembered herself.

There's something magnetic about a woman who is no longer trying to be someone else. The energy of self-possession cannot be replicated. It doesn't matter what she's wearing, how much she reveals or withholds, or whether anyone "gets" her. She is not for consumption. She is not trying to explain. She simply radiates. Because she's not acting like a goddess. She's being one.

And that doesn't mean she's always fierce or always composed. It means she is deeply, radically true. True to her instincts. True to her values. True to her mystery. She can cry in public and still command a room. She can rage in ritual and still be rooted in love. She can speak softly and still be the most powerful person present. There is no one mode. No singular look. Only coherence between who she is and how she moves.

Channeling myth into your identity does not require perfection. It requires presence. The more embodied you are, the more potent you become. You don't need to explain why you're changing. You don't need to convince anyone that your evolution is valid. Some people will sense your shift and fall away. Let them. That too is part of your initiation. Not everyone can walk with you where you're going. Not everyone is meant to.

The more archetypal you become, the more you activate others without even meaning to. You mirror their forgotten power. You trigger their hidden longing. You awaken something primal in those who thought they had themselves all figured out. You show what's possible when a woman stops editing herself. That's why some will be drawn to you and others will be disturbed by you. Both are signs you're doing it right.

Your mythic self is not a fixed persona. It's an evolving expression. It shifts with your seasons, your cycles, your rituals. You can be fire one day and ocean the next. You can disappear into the void and emerge brighter. You can reimagine yourself again and again without ever losing your core. That's what it means to live archetypally. You are not static. You are an unfolding symbol.

And in that unfolding, you become unforgettable. You stop being the woman who blends in. You become the one who lingers in memory, even after a brief encounter. You imprint. Not by trying harder, but by being more of who you truly are. You start to shape your life from the inside out. Not as a reaction, but as an act of design. You become the author of your own myth.

Not for validation. Not for performance. But because it is time. Time to stop playing small in a world that needs the full expression of who you are. Time to stop shrinking around those who fear the fire you carry. Time to walk into your life as a living myth, unapologetically alive, exquisitely complex, and unshakably magnetic.

Part II. The Magnetic Body

Your body is not separate from your power. It is the altar. The instrument. The language before language.

For generations, the body of the feminine has been treated as a problem to fix, an object to tame, or a tool to exploit. You've been taught to be desirable but not desiring. Visible but not too loud. Attractive but never in full ownership of your magnetism. This has created a split — between your mind and your instincts, between your sensuality and your worth, between how you feel and how you're told you should look.

But the truth is: the body is where your power *lives*.

This part of the journey is not about trying to "love your body" in a superficial or forced way. It's about remembering that your body is **already** sacred — not because it meets some ideal, but because it is yours. Because it carries memory. Because it responds to energy. Because it *knows* before your mind can catch up.

The Magnetic Body is not about fitting into anyone's idea of beauty. It is about embodying your own frequency so fully that your presence begins to speak for you. This isn't about being loud or dominant. It's about resonance. You begin to move differently. People feel you before they see you. And the more at home you become in your own skin, the more impossible it is to ignore you.

We'll explore the unconscious ways you've been taught to disconnect from your body — to distrust your hunger, to suppress your pleasure, to stay "in control." You'll uncover how your nervous system has been shaped by shame, how your sensuality has been commodified, and how your true magnetism has been locked behind layers of performance and repression. Then, we'll begin to unlock it.

This part of the path is deeply physical and deeply energetic. You'll meet the body not as something to "fix" but as something to re-inhabit, to listen to, to partner with. You'll begin to understand how to *charge* your body with presence instead of draining it through survival habits. You'll learn how movement, breath, voice, and erotic energy are not accessories to your power — they *are* the power.

You will not be asked to become someone else. You will not be asked to become more like "them."

You will be asked to return.

To the body that remembers your wildness.

To the voice that was silenced but never extinguished.

To the frequency that was always yours.

The Magnetic Body is not a performance. It is a state of being. One that radiates safety, seduction, and sovereignty in equal measure. One that doesn't just *look* powerful, but *feels* it — in the way you walk, the way you speak, the way you *choose*.

This is the re-embodiment of the Dark Femme.

Not the idea. Not the image.

The *real* return.

Let's begin.

Chapter 4: The Energetics of Presence

The Magnetic Field: How People Feel You Before You Speak

You've felt it before. That moment when someone walks into a room and everything shifts. No words. No performance. Just a presence that *lands*. People pause. Heads turn. The air becomes thick with something unspoken. You can't always explain it, but you feel it. It's visceral. And whether that person is speaking or silent, they've already made an impression.

This is the magnetic field. It's not imaginary. It's not just "vibes." It's the real, energetic signal your body emits — a result of how fully you are inhabiting yourself, how congruent your inner world is with your outer expression, and how safe you are in your own nervous system.

Most women are taught to focus on outer presentation: how to speak, how to move, how to act. But the deeper truth is that people respond to your energy *before* they respond to your words. In fact, the frequency you hold in your body sets the tone for every interaction you enter. If you are deeply self-contained, you feel magnetic. If you are fragmented or externally seeking, you feel off — even if your appearance is flawless.

Your magnetic field is not built by forcing confidence or faking charisma. It emerges when your inner landscape and outer expression are *aligned*. That's why two women can wear the same outfit, say the same line, and yet one is ignored while the other leaves people breathless. It's not the outfit. It's not even the words. It's the field.

What Shapes the Magnetic Field

Your magnetic field is not static. It shifts constantly in response to your nervous system, your emotions, your boundaries, and your connection to self. When you are regulated, grounded, and clear, your field expands. You become easier to feel. People are drawn in, not because you're "doing" anything, but because your energy communicates safety and charge at once. On the other hand, when you're in survival mode — fawning, performing, people-pleasing — your field contracts. Even if you're saying all the right things, people *sense* the disconnect. You may come across as sweet, likable,

56

even impressive, but not magnetic. Because true magnetism requires a level of embodiment that can't be faked.

This is why nervous system work is not a bonus. It's foundational. When your body doesn't feel safe, it shuts down the very qualities that create presence: breath, posture, voice, sensuality, clarity. You begin to dissociate, micromanage your image, or fall into old scripts. The body becomes stiff, the voice tight, the eyes dim.

But when you bring your awareness back into your body — into your hips, your chest, your breath — you start to generate charge. You aren't floating above yourself. You're *in* yourself. You can feel your spine. You can feel your feet on the ground. You're not waiting to be validated. You're listening to your own rhythm. That presence doesn't need to shout. It speaks before you open your mouth.

This is the difference between being noticed and being felt.

When someone is merely noticed, the attention they receive is fleeting. It relies on external cues — a loud voice, a bold move, a certain look. But when someone is *felt*, it creates a resonance that lingers. People remember how they felt in your presence long after the words are gone. And that is the essence of magnetism.

To cultivate this kind of resonance, your relationship with your body must shift from management to intimacy. It's not enough to train posture, mimic poise, or practice gestures. The field strengthens when you *listen* to your body, not when you override it. Your magnetism is a side effect of self-attunement. You have to feel yourself before others can feel you.

Most women are conditioned to be seen but not deeply felt. They know how to pose, how to flatter, how to entertain, but not how to anchor their energy. And when you're disconnected from your own energy, you become dependent on feedback to feel real. You look for cues in their faces, their tone, their interest. You adjust. You shrink. You amplify. You leave yourself. Magnetism is not a performance. It's an energetic invitation that says, *I'm home in myself. You're welcome to meet me here, but I'm not reaching outward to make it happen.*

The field becomes magnetic when there's nothing desperate about it. You are not trying to be felt. You simply are. You're not reaching out with need. You're radiating a frequency of self. And that self is unshakable because it's not built on external approval. It's rooted in embodied truth.

There is a weight to this kind of presence. A woman anchored in her field doesn't speak to be heard. She speaks because she has something to say. She doesn't touch to get attention. She touches because she feels connected. She doesn't rush to fill silence. Her stillness carries charge. That's why people lean in. That's why they remember her. She brings the fullness of her nervous system, her breath, her senses, her awareness into the space.

This isn't about being calm or still all the time. Aliveness and emotion can be magnetic too. The field doesn't require stoicism. It requires coherence. Even when you're angry, grieving, or fiery, if you're inside your experience instead of running from it, people feel you. They *trust* your energy, even if they don't consciously understand it.

You don't have to convince anyone when you're rooted in your own signal. The energy does the work. This is why so much of feminine magnetism has nothing to do with being louder or more dominant. In fact, it often looks like doing less — but with more presence. More intention. More charge behind every movement and word.

This is also why certain rituals, practices, and spaces that help you reconnect with your body's rhythms are not optional luxuries. They are part of how you refine your field. Breathwork, sensual movement, grounding, voicework, even stillness — these practices build your capacity to stay *with* yourself, even when the room is spinning or your mind wants to escape.

And the more you stay with yourself, the more undeniable your field becomes.

Your body is not an ornament. It's a transmitter. Every time you return to it, soften into it, breathe into it, you reclaim your signal. You expand the range of your expression. You stop waiting to be chosen and start existing as someone who cannot be overlooked. Not because you're trying to stand out. But because your energy is no longer dimmed, diluted, or outsourced. When you walk into a room holding that, people feel it. Before they even know your name.

Expanding Your Aura Through Intentional Embodiment

Your aura is not an abstract spiritual concept floating above your head. It is the felt expression of how fully you are *inhabiting* your body. It reflects how deeply you are rooted in your energy, how fluidly your life force is moving, and how safely your presence can hold its own in any environment. Expanding your aura is not about visualization techniques alone. It's about embodiment. And embodiment starts with choice.

You expand when you decide to be *in* your body. Fully. Not halfway. Not when it's convenient. Not only when things are calm or beautiful or sensual. True embodiment means staying present even when discomfort arises, even when old shame flares up, even when resistance whispers that it would be easier to float back into your head. Your aura shrinks when you abandon yourself. It expands when you remain.

This is not about being perfect. It's about being consistent. Your field grows stronger when your body learns that it can trust *you* to stay — to breathe through the awkwardness, to hold yourself through the emotion, to feel your sensations without flinching. When your nervous system registers that your own presence is safe, your energy begins to expand beyond your skin. That's what people feel when they meet you. Not just your face, not just your voice. But the space around you. The space you occupy with certainty. Not loudness. Not domination. But inner fullness. It doesn't demand. It magnetizes.

If your energy has felt small or collapsed in the past, it's not because something is wrong with you. It's because you learned to leave yourself. You learned to shrink, to accommodate, to disappear inside your own mind in moments of threat, rejection, or pressure. You learned to separate from the sensations in your chest, your belly, your pelvis. You dissociated from your power because it didn't feel safe to own it.

But that can shift. Not through willpower, not through force, but through gentle, daily reclamation. When you walk, you walk *in* your hips. When you speak, you speak *from* your belly. When you look into someone's eyes, you look *with* your whole presence — not from a distant, guarded self.

This is intentional embodiment. You are not passively moving through the world. You are animating your body from the inside out. You are aware of your spine, your breath, the ground beneath your feet. And that awareness begins to charge your field. It builds a kind of energetic density that others feel even before you speak.

What most people call confidence is often just a coherent field. It's the effect of a person who is not leaking energy, not posturing, not seeking permission to exist. A person who is *inhabiting* herself. Not occasionally. Not selectively. But as a way of life.

Embodiment, when practiced with intention, doesn't just restore presence. It becomes influence. It softens resistance in others without needing to argue, justify, or prove. This is because your nervous system begins to co-regulate the room. The moment you enter a space grounded and full in your body, you offer something few people realize they're craving: coherence.

Most people live in their heads, fractured and fragmented. Their energy drifts, their attention scatters, their presence flickers like a weak signal. But when someone walks in fully seated in themselves, it creates a quiet authority that doesn't need to speak over anyone. That stillness is power. It reorders dynamics without force.

You become more than what you say. You become a frequency that others feel. And because it's rare, it becomes magnetic. This is the secret behind the presence of women who seem to shift the energy of a space without doing anything performative. They are not seeking to be seen. They are being. They do not chase impact. They *are* impact. Not because they are louder, but because they are anchored.

Intentional embodiment means you are constantly transmitting a signal. Not in the sense of trying to be "on" or curated. In fact, any attempt to perform will collapse your field. What transmits is *realness* — a nervous system that is regulated, a body that is fully inhabited, and a woman who does not abandon herself to gain favor, praise, or approval.

To sustain this, your body must learn that it is safe to take up space. Not only physically, but emotionally, sexually, energetically. You can't fake that. You cultivate it through practice. Through breath. Through movement. Through sensation. Through holding your center when you would normally leave yourself.

As your field strengthens, something else happens. You stop absorbing everyone else's chaos. You stop internalizing projections. You stop taking responsibility for other people's discomfort. Not by hardening, but by staying anchored. Your field becomes not only a transmission but also a container. What is not yours bounces off. What is meant for you comes in clean.

This is where discernment sharpens. You no longer dilute your truth for comfort. You no longer twist yourself into someone else's image of acceptability. The more you embody, the more the external world becomes a mirror. Not a dictator. Not a measuring stick. A mirror. You read it without reacting. You sense what is aligned, and you adjust from the inside, not from fear.

None of this is instant. It is subtle. Daily. Sensory. But over time, your aura becomes an extension of your integrity. You walk into a room, and without saying a word, people feel you've done the work. They may not know what they're sensing, but they sense *something*. A field that is not seeking. A field that is full. A woman who has come home to herself, not just once, but again and again.

And that kind of presence is unforgettable. Not because it screams. But because it stays. It holds. It remains long after you've walked away.

Daily Practices to Turn on Your Feminine Charge

Feminine charge is not something you put on like makeup. It's something you awaken, feed, and embody through the rhythm of your everyday life. This isn't about seduction tricks or exaggerated femininity. It's about activating the energy that naturally lives in you but has likely been dimmed by over-efforting, constant output, and emotional shutdown.

The truth is, most women are disconnected from this charge not because they lack it, but because their nervous system has been trained to suppress it in order to survive. Expression became dangerous. Desire became shameful. Receptivity became weakness. So the very circuits that light up your feminine essence have gone numb.

To turn them back on, you need daily touchpoints that bring you back into your body, your breath, your emotions, and your senses. The feminine doesn't thrive in speed. She needs space. She needs to feel. She needs to be felt. And this doesn't require hours of rituals or exotic tools. It begins with awareness. With intention. With choosing to shift out of autopilot and into aliveness.

This is why consistency matters more than intensity. You don't need a massive transformation. You need a regular return to yourself. And that return happens in the mundane: how you move, how you breathe, how you dress, how you notice the texture of your day.

One of the most overlooked doorways into feminine charge is sensation. Not thinking about how you feel, but actually *feeling it*. Letting sensation flood your body without rushing to label or fix it. This is where suppressed energy begins to move again. Shame softens. Desire stirs. Playfulness returns. You begin to inhabit yourself more fully, not as a performance, but as a presence.

Start by asking your body, not your mind: What do I want to feel today? What texture does my energy crave? Is it softness? Is it fire? Is it depth? Is it sensuality? And then find a way to *invite* that energy in, rather than force it.

The feminine awakens through invitation, not discipline. Through pleasure, not pressure. This doesn't mean living without structure. It means choosing structure that honors your cyclical nature, not one that tries to dominate it. The practices that turn on your charge are the ones that make you feel more *you*. They reconnect you with your erotic aliveness, your creative flow, your emotional range, and your physical power. And they don't have to look like anyone else's. What matters is not the appearance of the practice, but the *energy* it unlocks in you.

This is why it's not about following a perfect routine. It's about learning to tune into your internal landscape and respond. Some days, activating your charge might mean dancing. Other days, it might mean crying. Or resting. Or laughing uncontrollably. Or saying no. The deeper you go, the more you realize this charge is not a fixed state, but a fluid current. And your job is not to control it, but to ride it with reverence.

Let's now look at how you can begin weaving this into your everyday life, not as another task, but as a living pulse that infuses everything you touch. What this asks of you is intimacy with your own energy. Not performance, not striving, but presence. This means noticing the moments when your breath tightens, when your shoulders lift with tension, when your voice flattens to sound agreeable. These are the cues that you've slipped into disconnection. And you don't need to judge yourself for it. You just need to come back.

Returning can be as simple as placing your hand on your lower belly and breathing into it. Or swaying your hips while waiting for your coffee to brew. Or slipping into clothes that awaken something sensual in your skin, even if no one sees you. These are not small things. They are recalibrations. Each time you do them, you signal to your nervous system that it is safe to feel, to take up space, to move with rhythm instead of rigidity.

Movement is one of the fastest ways to return to charge. Not exercise, necessarily, but *movement with intention*. Let your body lead for a few minutes without choreography. Let your hips speak. Let your shoulders soften. Let your breath guide the tempo. The goal is not beauty. The goal is aliveness. When you move this way, you don't just release energy. You reclaim it.

Another powerful access point is your voice. Most women have silenced their real tone to sound more acceptable. To be pleasing. To avoid being "too much." But sound is primal. Vibrational. It stirs energy awake in the body. Try humming low in your throat. Try making sound without words. Moans, sighs, growls. Let them rise without censorship. Your voice is a portal. Use it to open energy that words alone cannot.

Touch, too, is sacred. Self-touch isn't only for arousal. It's for presence. Run your fingers over your own skin like you would if you were discovering

63

yourself for the first time. Not with urgency, but with curiosity. Let your touch say, "I see you. I feel you. You're here." When your body feels adored by *you*, it stops waiting for someone else to give it permission to come alive. And perhaps the most underestimated practice of all: emotional honesty. Letting yourself feel the full spectrum of your emotion, without spiritualizing it, minimizing it, or bypassing it. The feminine thrives in truth, and truth is not always pretty. Sometimes your charge gets activated by rage. By grief. By heartbreak. That, too, is part of your magnetism. When you stop making your emotions wrong, they start to move. And when they move, so does your power.

None of this works if done from a place of control. These are not tools to manipulate energy. They are invitations. The more gently you hold them, the more they open. The more you listen, the more they speak. Your feminine charge cannot be forced. It must be *invited* to return.

Let that return become your devotion. Not as something you check off a list, but as a sacred agreement with yourself. That no matter how loud the world becomes, you will keep coming back to your own pulse. That your body will not be treated as a machine. That your aliveness will not be sacrificed for productivity. That your magnetism will be nourished, not hidden.

This is the feminine in practice. This is power that doesn't scream but makes the room lean in. This is the kind of charge that does not burn out. It *builds*, quietly, consistently, until one day you look in the mirror and realize you are no longer waiting to be chosen. You have chosen *yourself*, and everything else is drawn to that.

Chapter 5: Sensual Power, Not Sexual Performance

Why Embodiment Trumps External Validation

There is a kind of confidence that doesn't need to be seen to exist. It doesn't need compliments, comments, or double-taps to be real. It's the kind of confidence that lives inside the body — not because someone else confirmed it, but because you've felt it ripple through your cells. This is what embodiment gives you. Not the illusion of confidence, but its root. The unshakeable kind that exists even when no one is watching.

External validation is addictive because it's immediate. A look, a message, an approval — they hit quickly. And in a world that teaches women to base their worth on how wanted they are, how admired, how chosen, it's no surprise that many are conditioned to seek their reflection in someone else's eyes. But no matter how much you chase it, external validation is a moving target. It requires performance. It shifts with trends, moods, opinions. And the more you rely on it, the more fragile your sense of self becomes.

Embodiment, on the other hand, isn't loud. It doesn't beg to be seen. It doesn't need to impress. But when you walk into a room with it, people *feel* you before you speak. You're not just wearing confidence. You're *inhabiting* it. There's weight to your presence, a coherence between your energy and your actions that makes you magnetic. It's the difference between posing as powerful and being power.

The body never lies. It knows when you're performing. It knows when you're pretending to be confident while feeling hollow inside. And so does everyone else, even if they can't articulate it. That's why someone who doesn't fit conventional beauty standards can be the most magnetic woman in the room, while someone who checks every superficial box still feels forgettable. Magnetism comes from congruence. When what you feel and what you express are aligned, the world can't look away.

That congruence begins in the body. Not in your thoughts, not in your affirmations, but in the way you breathe, move, and *own* your space. It's in the way you let yourself feel emotion without tensing up or bracing for judgment. It's in the way you allow your sensuality to be present without apology or shame. When you are in your body, you are no longer watching yourself from the outside. You are *being*. And that is the most powerful state you can inhabit.

This doesn't mean you'll never crave being seen or desired. You're human. But there's a difference between sharing your radiance and leaking it to get scraps of approval. When you are embodied, you can enjoy being witnessed without being dependent on it. You can receive a compliment with grace without needing it to feel secure. You can flirt without attachment, post without performing, seduce without scrambling for confirmation. Because you're no longer waiting to be told you're enough. You're already living from that place.

This is why embodiment is not just about body language or posture. It's about *reclaiming your own experience* as the source of your truth. It's deciding that your felt sense of aliveness matters more than how others respond to it. That the energy moving through your body is more meaningful than the feedback loop of approval. You stop outsourcing your identity and start rooting it in something no one can take from you.

What shifts when you stop needing the world to mirror your worth is that your actions become clean. You're no longer trying to control perception. You're expressing what is real. This is where true magnetism arises — not from being perfect, but from being honest. Not from playing a role, but from fully living your reality. And this kind of presence cannot be manufactured. It can only be cultivated from within.

There's a sacred power in knowing that your value does not rise or fall based on how others respond to you. That your worth is not up for negotiation, not filtered through someone else's gaze, not determined by numbers, comments, or attention. That clarity comes from being anchored in your body, because the body is where your truth lives. The more deeply you inhabit it, the harder it becomes to be manipulated by approval or rejection. External validation hooks into wounds. It flares up when the girl inside you still believes love must be earned, still equates beauty with safety, still confuses performance with connection. It rewards the mask and punishes the real. And every time you bend yourself for praise, you move a little further from your own center. The cost of being validated for a false self is that the true self remains starved.

66

But when you lead with embodiment, something radical happens. You begin to taste freedom. You realize you don't have to shapeshift to be desirable. You don't have to curate yourself to be enough. You don't have to make yourself smaller or sweeter or more palatable to be loved. You begin to live as someone who belongs to herself. And that presence is unforgettable.

This isn't about abandoning beauty, seduction, or the joy of being seen. It's about making sure they serve your wholeness rather than hijack it. Embodiment lets you enjoy attention without being enslaved by it. You can choose to be expressive, sensual, radiant — but from a place of overflow, not emptiness. Not because you're trying to earn a response, but because your being is already full and cannot help but shine.

When you live in this state, people feel the difference. They don't just see you. They *sense* you. There's a coherence that runs through your gestures, your tone, your silence. You don't have to speak louder or try harder. You don't need to dominate a room or prove anything. You simply exist in a way that others feel drawn to. That's the magnetism of embodiment. It bypasses logic. It speaks to the nervous system. It's primal.

And ironically, it's in this state — when you're no longer chasing validation — that you often receive it the most. But now, it lands differently. You don't cling to it. You don't mold yourself around it. You let it move through you like wind, without needing it to define anything. You can take it in, appreciate it, and still stay rooted in your own ground.

This shift also rewires your boundaries. When your sense of value lives in your own body, you stop tolerating dynamics that drain or distort it. You stop trying to be understood by people who only relate to your surface. You stop handing your energy to those who only respond when you perform. Embodiment sharpens your discernment. It helps you feel the subtle shifts when your truth contracts or expands. And it gives you the courage to move accordingly, even when it means walking alone.

There is nothing passive about this way of being. It's a reclamation. A returning. A deep, cellular remembrance of who you are when you stop outsourcing your power. The more you live here, the more naturally you begin to attract what is aligned — not because you're playing the game better, but because you're no longer playing it at all.

You've stepped off the stage. You've left the need to be chosen. And in that space, what rises is not just power, but peace. The peace of being whole, witnessed or not. The peace of knowing that you are enough, not someday, but now. The peace of a woman who no longer performs, because she has finally come home to herself.

Awakening the Senses to Rewire the Nervous System

The nervous system is the hidden architecture of your experience. It determines whether your body feels like a safe place to live or a battlefield of survival. Whether you meet the world with openness or bracing. Whether pleasure expands you or overloads you. And for most women raised in a world that demands control, performance, and protection, the nervous system has learned to compress itself around danger — even when there is none. It stays guarded, braced, frozen. It doesn't trust softness. It flinches at slowness. It rejects too much sensation.

This is not a failure. It's an adaptation. But it cannot be healed through thought alone. You cannot affirm your way into safety, nor can you analyze your way into regulation. The nervous system speaks the language of sensation. It responds to what it feels, not what you think. And this is where your senses become the most powerful doorway to healing.

To awaken the senses is not to indulge or escape. It's to retrain the body to receive without shutting down. To notice what's present without speeding past it. To let pleasure in without guilt or fear. The more you practice this, the more your nervous system learns that it's safe to soften. Safe to expand. Safe to feel.

Many women are disconnected from their sensory body because they've been taught to override it. Taught to numb through productivity. Taught to prioritize appearance over experience. Taught to intellectualize everything instead of living it. But embodiment cannot happen from the neck up. You cannot access your feminine magnetism while your body is numb, your senses dulled, and your breath shallow.

Waking up the senses is a reclamation. It's a way of coming home to a self that is fully alive, even in stillness. It begins with noticing: the texture of fabric on your skin, the weight of your body in a chair, the scent in the air, the rhythm of your breath. These are not small things. They are doorways. Each sensory cue is a way to root yourself in the now, which is the only place the nervous system can regulate. The future is too fast. The past is too heavy. The present is where healing lives.

And in that present moment, your body holds immense wisdom. It knows what it needs to relax. It knows what kind of touch melts your defenses. It knows the pace at which it wants to be approached. But most women never ask. They've learned to skip over the body's signals, or worse, to mistrust them. They've learned to fake arousal, to smile when uncomfortable, to say yes when their cells are screaming no. Reversing this conditioning takes more than awareness. It takes practice.

This practice is not about perfection. It's about attunement. Learning to tune into your body like a finely calibrated instrument. Listening for its yes. Respecting its no. And most importantly, allowing your senses to be reawakened without agenda. Not to perform, not to seduce, not to be productive — but simply to feel. That alone is a revolution.

Let's begin where it matters most. Not in theory, but in direct experience. You don't need to change your life overnight. You don't need to force open the doors. You just need to begin listening again.

Sensory Anchoring: A Practice for Nervous System Safety

Choose one sense at a time. Not to overwhelm or flood the body with sensation, but to create a safe, steady anchor point. If touch is the easiest, begin there. Let your fingertips explore the softness of a scarf, the firmness of wood, the cool surface of stone. Let your body feel without judgment. Your mind might try to assign meaning, to analyze or label. That's fine. Let it pass. Come back to the texture. The weight. The temperature. Let it ground you.

If sound feels more accessible, drop into the layers. The hum of a refrigerator. The rustle of leaves. The faint buzz in your ears. Let your nervous system hear what it normally tunes out. Not to interpret, but to receive. You are training your body to notice without bracing. To stay present without running. This is nervous system healing. Not in theory, but in the language it understands.

The more consistently you practice this, the more safety your body will begin to associate with presence. What once felt dangerous — stillness, closeness, pleasure — becomes tolerable. Then nourishing. Then magnetic. You will feel the shift not only inside your skin but in how the world responds to you. Others will sense your coherence before you speak. They'll feel your groundedness without needing explanation. This is the hidden power of a woman who is sensually present. She doesn't manipulate energy. She embodies it.

If emotions rise as you re-enter your sensory body, honor them. Often, the numbness was protecting something tender — a memory, a grief, a wound.

Let the body express in its own time. Tears, movement, stillness, even laughter. Don't chase sensation with force. Don't try to make it into a performance. This is not about being more "feminine" for someone else. It's about remembering that you are a living, breathing, feeling being. That your nervous system doesn't need to be braced in survival mode forever. That you get to feel deeply and be safe at the same time.

Many women fear that awakening their senses will make them too sensitive, too emotional, too overwhelmed. But the opposite is true. The more you allow safe sensation, the more resilient you become. Regulation is not about flatness. It's about flexibility. The ability to move between states without getting stuck. The ability to feel intensity and return to calm. The ability to stay present through both ecstasy and discomfort.

This is the essence of a magnetic nervous system. It doesn't reject the world, nor does it absorb everything blindly. It filters, calibrates, chooses. And it does so from a body that is awake, not one that's frozen in outdated patterns. Awakening the senses is not just a healing tool. It's a recalibration of identity. You stop being the woman who needs to be numb to survive, and become the one who can feel everything without being undone.

Your presence shifts. Your timing slows. You stop rushing into conversations, proving your worth, or over-explaining your existence. You enter a room and feel its texture. You walk into relationships with awareness rather than reaction. Your voice lowers. Your energy expands. And people respond to what they can't explain. They feel something before you speak. That's the nervous system transmitting your truth without words.

You don't need to fix your energy. You need to inhabit it. That begins with coming back into your body, one sense at a time. The rest will follow.

The Art of Walking, Speaking, and Touching With Intention

There is a difference between moving through the world and being moved by your own energy as you do. One passes unnoticed. The other rearranges a room. Intention is what separates them. It's not about performing a version of femininity. It's about becoming attuned to your own impact. When a woman walks, speaks, and touches with embodied presence, she sends ripples through the field. Without force. Without excess. Without needing to explain herself.

Many women have been taught to either shrink or exaggerate. We dim our light to be liked. Or we overexpress to be seen. Both are compensations for a missing center. Intentional movement is what brings you back to that center. It's not mechanical. It's not about posture or etiquette. It's about integrity between your inner state and your outer expression. Your body becomes congruent with your energy. Your presence starts to speak before your mouth does.

Walking as Transmission

Your walk is not just locomotion. It is language. It tells people how to treat you. It tells your nervous system how safe and solid you are. Most people walk as if trying to get somewhere else. As if their body is just the vehicle, not the message. When you slow your pace just slightly and become aware of each step, something shifts. You stop chasing time. You stop leaking energy. You start anchoring.

Feel the heel touch the ground first. Then the ball. Then the toes. Let your hips move, even if subtly. Don't control it. Just allow the natural sway of your pelvis to return. Soften your knees. Let your chest lift slightly, not in rigidity but in quiet authority. And most importantly, let your awareness drop into your lower body. Into your hips. Into your thighs. Into the parts of you that have been taught to disconnect in the name of politeness or shame.

This is not a performance. This is you re-inhabiting your body. Every time you walk with intention, you're telling the world, and yourself: I am not in a rush to earn my worth. I am not escaping this moment. I am here. Fully.

Speaking From the Root

Words are spells. And yet many women have been conditioned to speak as if asking permission. Our sentences trail upward, unsure. We pad our truths with qualifiers to make them more palatable. We apologize for taking up space before we've even begun. Intentional speech doesn't mean being loud or assertive in a masculine sense. It means letting your voice arise from a grounded place in your body. Not your head. Not your throat. But deeper. Before speaking, feel your feet. Feel your breath drop into your belly. Let silence be part of your rhythm. Let pauses become sacred. Don't rush to fill space. Space is part of your presence.

When your voice aligns with your inner knowing, people hear you differently. It's not just what you say, it's where you're saying it from. A woman who speaks with embodied intention doesn't need to explain herself over and over. Her words land because they carry the frequency of her own authority.

Let's pause here before we deepen into the power of touch — not as something external or seductive, but as a language of presence and energy exchange. The next layer will explore how touch, when used with intentional awareness, becomes one of the most powerful tools for influence, healing, and energetic clarity.

Touch is one of the most misunderstood aspects of feminine power. It's often reduced to seduction, manipulation, or caretaking. But when you bring awareness to your touch, you begin to realize it is neither tool nor transaction. It is transmission. Every time you place your hand on someone's arm, brush past someone, adjust your necklace, or run your fingers along your own skin, you are sending a message. The question is: are you conscious of what that message is?

Intentional touch begins with touch turned inward. Before you extend energy outward, you must be attuned to the sensations within your own body. Most women have been taught to ignore their tactile experience until it is needed for someone else's benefit. But the woman who knows how she wants to be touched, who regularly touches her own skin with presence and reverence, becomes magnetic. Not because she's trying to be. But because her body is already awake.

Start by reclaiming self-touch in the most ordinary ways. When you moisturize your legs, do it as if you are tending to sacred ground. When you run your fingers through your hair, do it like you are reminding yourself that you belong here. These small moments of embodied awareness build an energy field that others feel, even if they can't name it. You are not asking for attention. You are rooted in sensation. You are broadcasting presence.

When you touch another person, pause for a fraction of a second. Let your energy meet theirs. Don't rush. Don't default. Whether it's a handshake, a kiss on the cheek, or a hand resting on someone's shoulder, bring your full awareness into that contact. What do you intend to communicate? Groundedness? Warmth? Authority? Mystery? Connection? Your touch will carry the frequency you choose.

This practice does not require performance. It requires presence. And that presence, when consistent, begins to rewire the nervous system. Not just yours, but also of those around you. You become a walking reset point. People find themselves relaxing in your presence without knowing why. You offer no apology for your aliveness. You become an invitation for others to drop into their own bodies.

True feminine power is never frantic. It doesn't grasp. It doesn't prove. It moves with the quiet certainty of one who knows she belongs. Walking, speaking, and touching with intention is how you embody that knowing. You are no longer a concept. You are no longer a role. You are a signal. And that signal is felt far before it is understood.

This level of embodiment also creates discernment. You stop engaging with people or situations that drain you, because you are too attuned to how your body responds. You don't override your sensations to maintain politeness. You begin to trust your own felt intelligence more than anyone's opinion. That alone makes you magnetic. Not in a performative way, but in a way that is undeniably real.

People are drawn to what they feel they have lost. A woman who walks with presence, speaks with her full breath, and touches with sacred awareness reminds others of what is possible within themselves. She becomes unforgettable, not because she demands attention, but because she embodies a kind of freedom that few allow themselves to access.

This is not about perfection. This is about returning to your body, again and again, until it becomes your home. Until every step you take, every word you speak, and every touch you offer becomes a living prayer to your own power. That is the art. And that is what creates the kind of presence that transforms rooms, relationships, and realities.

Chapter 6: Strategic Unavailability and Feminine Polarity

How to Use Distance to Create Desire

Desire thrives in space. Not in absence, not in silence meant to punish, but in space that breathes with intention. The feminine is often portrayed as endlessly available, nurturing, ever-giving. But true feminine magnetism understands the power of withdrawal. Not as manipulation, but as sacred conservation. She does not always rush to close the gap. She knows that distance, when conscious, pulls desire toward her like a tide responding to the moon.

Most people are terrified of space. They associate it with abandonment, rejection, or being forgotten. But this fear is born from disconnection, not truth. In reality, distance is where longing lives. It's where imagination awakens. It's where someone begins to feel your absence not as emptiness, but as a signal of your value. If you are always in reach, if your energy is always available on demand, there is nothing to yearn for, nothing to chase, nothing to feel pulled toward.

To embody the art of sacred distance, you must first be deeply anchored in yourself. You cannot use space as a strategy unless you're comfortable inhabiting it. That means no frantic checking, no silent hoping, no anxious monitoring. Distance is not about waiting. It's about living. Fully. The feminine does not shrink while unseen. She expands.

When you step back with presence, you're not disappearing. You're creating contrast. You are giving the other person the opportunity to notice the difference between your presence and your absence. That contrast is what allows desire to rise. Without it, everything becomes neutral. Flat. Predictable.

This does not mean withholding affection, communication, or care to provoke a reaction. That is rooted in fear, not power. Sacred distance is not punitive. It is magnetic because it honors your wholeness. You are not using absence as a game. You are simply not afraid to stop filling every space.

This also applies to how you show up energetically. Sometimes your body is physically present, but your energy is leaking out in every direction. You're overly accessible. Over-explaining. Over-clarifying. You leave no room for curiosity because you're constantly trying to manage perception. In doing so, you dilute your impact.

A woman rooted in her feminine charge knows when to pull back. She knows how to sit in silence without needing to break it. She knows how to pause before responding. She knows how to leave a room while still being felt in it. That is not coldness. That is mastery.

Creating desire through distance begins with trusting that your energy is potent enough to echo. You do not need to constantly prove your worth through performance or presence. You let your absence become part of your signal. And you trust that the right people will feel the pull, not because you demanded it, but because you allowed it.

Many women fear that if they stop reaching, they'll be forgotten. But the truth is, when you stop reaching from a place of fear, you make space for attraction to happen on its own. You make room for others to move toward you. You invite polarity back into the dynamic. And it is polarity that creates spark.

We live in a world obsessed with immediacy. Quick replies, constant updates, instant validation. But desire does not move at that pace. Desire is slow. It lingers. It needs air. When you can resist the urge to fill every moment, when you can trust in the power of your stillness, you become rare. And rarity awakens longing.

Distance becomes magnetic when it's born from inner fullness, not emptiness. When a woman pulls back from a centered place, her absence holds structure. It signals to the world that her energy is not casual. She is not constantly available because she is devoted elsewhere—within. Her time, her attention, her emotional availability are not open fields anyone can run through. They are sacred, curated, and consciously offered.

This kind of distance sharpens awareness. The people around her begin to notice what they had been unconsciously consuming. They feel the shift. And in that pause, reflection begins. Real desire is not sparked by pressure. It's born in the space where one has time to feel. You are not just giving others a chance to miss you. You are letting them feel the contrast between

76

presence and absence, connection and quiet. That contrast is where energetic impact multiplies.

To hold this space well, you must become comfortable with discomfort. You have to be able to feel the pull to reach out and still choose not to. Not out of pride, but out of devotion to your own energetic integrity. If your desire to close the distance comes from anxiety, it will never create attraction. It will only soothe your nerves momentarily, while slowly eroding polarity.

Polarity thrives when both people are rooted in self. The feminine creates space by softening, by leaning back, by trusting. Not passively, not with resentment, but with power. She chooses herself while leaving the door open. Not wide open. Just enough that if someone has the desire and capacity to move toward her, they can. But they must choose it. That's where the magnetism begins.

This does not mean playing games or pretending to be indifferent. Your warmth, your affection, your vulnerability are still powerful tools. But when you layer them over a foundation of healthy energetic distance, they become irresistible. A woman who knows how to give affection without chasing, to reveal herself without clinging, to open without collapsing, is unforgettable. Intentional distance also allows you to observe clearly. When you are constantly filling every space, you cannot see how someone truly responds to your presence. But when you pause, when you leave room, their behavior reveals itself. Who moves toward you when you stop moving first? Who stays connected without you holding all the weight? These moments give you clarity not just about others, but about your own patterns too.

The practice of conscious distance is ultimately about boundaries without defense. You are not armoring yourself. You are allowing enough space between you and others that your presence retains meaning. You are willing to be missed. You are willing to let tension rise. You are even willing to let some things fall away. Because what remains after the space is honored is what was meant to stay.

In relationships, distance should not feel like punishment. It should feel like mystery. Not confusion, not mixed signals, but the kind of spaciousness that leaves someone leaning in. That leaning in is what builds emotional tension, the kind that becomes desire. And that kind of desire cannot be manufactured. It must be allowed.

When you master the art of sacred distance, you stop fearing loss. You stop managing every interaction. You stop performing for closeness. And in doing so, you become the very thing that draws others near. Not because you demanded their attention. But because you stood still long enough for your signal to be felt through the noise.

This is not about becoming cold or detached. It's about presence with boundaries. Warmth with discernment. Openness with self-trust. It's about knowing that your energy is a current, and that pulling it back, even slightly, sends ripples through any space you've once entered. The woman who holds that power needs no explanation. She becomes unforgettable. Not through her effort, but through her absence.

Feminine Polarity vs Masculine Hustle

Modern life rewards the masculine hustle. The grind, the goal-setting, the constant doing. From the moment we wake up, there's a cultural script that whispers: produce more, be efficient, dominate your schedule, conquer your to-do list. Success is measured by motion. Value is defined by how much you achieve before noon. The world celebrates the masculine rhythm of linear progress: plan, execute, win.

But the feminine doesn't move in a straight line. She flows. She expands, contracts, and spirals inward before she bursts outward. Her power lies not in relentless doing but in magnetic being. Feminine polarity is not laziness or passivity. It's a completely different current. It pulls rather than pushes. It draws in rather than chases. It waits, not from weakness, but from wisdom. And that waiting, that quiet potency, often goes unrecognized in a culture addicted to speed.

Feminine polarity lives in the body, not in the mind's strategy. It's about energetic presence, emotional depth, and embodied truth. A woman in her feminine does not need to prove her worth. She does not strive to be chosen. She does not seek validation through her productivity. She knows that her value is inherent, not earned through exhaustion. She holds space rather than filling it. She inspires action, but she is not driven by the same fuel as the masculine.

This is where the distortion happens for so many women. We are taught to be desirable but also independent. Soft but also strong. Receptive but also assertive. In this confusion, many women unconsciously abandon their feminine magnetism to survive in masculine spaces. They grind. They push. They achieve. And though they might succeed externally, they feel numb internally. Disconnected from their bodies, their intuition, their radiance.

The masculine hustle is not wrong. It is a sacred energy, necessary in its time and place. The problem arises when it becomes the default mode, when there is no balance, no return, no surrender. When a woman lives only in her hustle, she starts to burn out not because she's incapable, but because she is living out of alignment with her deepest essence. Her nervous system tightens. Her sensuality fades. Her inner world goes silent.

Feminine polarity is a reclamation of a different way. It is not about doing nothing. It is about doing from a different state of being. It's about inspired action that rises from intuition, not obligation. It's about leaning back and letting life come to you, without guilt. It's about choosing ease not because you're weak, but because you've remembered how powerful softness can be.

A woman in her feminine polarity becomes magnetic not by trying to be seen, but by being deeply connected to herself. Her emotions are not a problem to fix but a landscape to explore. Her pleasure is not a reward for hard work, but a compass guiding her deeper into her truth. Her energy is not fragmented, chasing results, but coherent, radiating wholeness.

This polarity is not just personal. It's relational. When a woman drops into her feminine, she creates space for the masculine to rise around her. Not because she manipulates, but because polarity is a law of nature. Opposites attract when both poles are fully owned. If she holds the feminine with depth, she invites a deeper masculine to meet her. But when she abandons her essence to control, chase, or prove, the polarity dissolves.

There is power in both poles. But they must be honored differently. Feminine power is not about domination. It's about devotion. It is not frantic. It is fierce in its stillness. And it does not compete with the masculine hustle. It balances it. Without that balance, both energies lose their brilliance.

When a woman leads with her masculine for too long, her body keeps score. Fatigue sets in that no caffeine can fix. Her cycle might shift, her libido might fade, her sleep becomes shallow. She wakes up feeling like she's already behind. The constant doing leaves no space for simply being. Even her relationships begin to reflect this imbalance. She might attract men who lean back, avoid leadership, or are unclear in their direction. The outer mirrors the inner.

In contrast, when she allows herself to live from her feminine, something begins to soften and recalibrate. Her nervous system relaxes, and with it, her magnetism begins to return. She becomes more receptive, more grounded, more alive in her senses. There's a quiet glow that emerges, the kind you can't fake. She stops trying to be everything at once and remembers that her presence is enough.

This isn't about rejecting the masculine within her. She still has goals. She still takes action. But she no longer sacrifices her feminine energy to achieve them. She lets herself flow toward results instead of dragging herself forward. She honors her natural rhythms. She knows when to lean back and when to lean in. She no longer forces herself to match a pace that isn't hers just to prove she's worthy of being taken seriously.

The deeper truth is that feminine polarity is not weaker than masculine hustle. It's simply different. The world needs both. But when one dominates the other for too long, distortion happens. The feminine becomes disconnected, anxious, and self-suppressing. The masculine becomes rigid, aggressive, and disconnected from emotion. Balance is not just spiritual, it's biological. It brings the nervous system into harmony and allows energy to flow in a way that nourishes instead of drains.

In intimacy, this polarity is the difference between a flat dynamic and a charged one. Masculine hustle doesn't create erotic tension. Polarity does. It's not about performance, but about presence. When a woman roots into her feminine, she becomes a safe space for emotional intimacy and a source of deep inspiration. She doesn't need to impress, overgive, or micromanage. Her power is in her ability to feel, to intuit, to trust herself even in the unknown.

She draws people in because she's connected to something deeper than approval. She's not afraid to pause. To listen. To change her mind. She lets silence speak. She allows herself to be seen without armoring. That vulnerability, when rooted in inner safety, becomes irresistible. It tells the world: I am here, I am whole, I am not chasing anything.

This is what makes feminine polarity so rare and so powerful. It's not loud, but it is unmistakable. It does not compete. It does not demand. It simply is. And from that place, she creates a different kind of success. One that feels aligned. One that feels nourishing. One that doesn't require her to trade her softness for strength.

The invitation is not to reject your drive or your ambition. It's to meet them with discernment. Ask yourself not just what you are doing, but *how* you are doing it. Are you trying to force the outcome? Or are you attuned to your deeper rhythm? Are you chasing from lack, or allowing from fullness?

The feminine is not a costume to put on. It is your essence to come home to. And when you do, you don't lose power. You step into the kind of power that no one can give or take away. It moves through you. It breathes with you. And it begins to shape a life that feels like truth.

Making Space for the Chase Without Manipulation

There is an ancient pull within the masculine to pursue and an equally sacred pull within the feminine to be pursued. Not from ego, but from energy. Not from a place of strategy, but from polarity. When this dance unfolds naturally, it creates magnetic tension, one that pulls the other in without needing to chase or perform. But modern conditioning has blurred this balance. Many women have been taught that making space for the chase is either manipulative or passive, and so they step in and try to control the outcome instead of magnetizing it.

Yet to allow space for pursuit is not weakness. It's not trickery. It's wisdom. The art lies in how you hold your energy, not in playing games. You are not withholding to create lack, you are holding your wholeness without collapsing. There is no need to pretend you don't care, no need to drop hints or disappear. That's manipulation. True feminine magnetism is about creating space with intention, not to provoke insecurity, but to protect your own clarity and power.

The masculine craves a current to follow. He seeks something to move toward, not something that clings or chases. When you overinvest too early, overexplain your feelings, or try to speed up connection out of fear, you short-circuit the polarity. You move into the space he is meant to fill. You close the gap before he feels the tension to cross it. In doing so, you rob yourself of the very dynamic your feminine energy was meant to ignite.

The feminine does not chase, but that doesn't mean she sits still. She cultivates herself. She becomes fully engaged with her own life, her own pleasure, her own expression. She doesn't wait to be chosen. She is already chosen by herself. She lives in a way that honors her radiance without apology. That creates space. And that space is the invitation.

Men feel this. They feel when your attention is rooted in yourself, not in their response. They feel when you are moving from fullness, not need. That's what makes the space potent. It isn't empty. It's filled with your essence. It doesn't demand attention. It draws it.

Creating this space means letting go of the need to control what the other person thinks or feels. You stop trying to be understood at every moment. You don't force conversations when you feel uncertain. You don't overshare to gain closeness. Instead, you remain open but grounded.

Expressive but anchored. It's a balance between receptivity and discernment. Between softness and boundaries.

This space also allows you to observe. To feel how someone moves toward you without being swept up in fantasy or overanalysis. You watch what they choose without needing to push or pull. You let their behavior reveal their intent. And you trust yourself enough to let it be seen.

The chase isn't about playing hard to get. It's about being deeply connected to your own worth, so you don't have to negotiate for love or closeness. You know that real connection cannot be forced. It must unfold. And it often unfolds through contrast — through the absence that invites presence. Through pauses that create longing. Through moments of mystery that allow discovery.

That kind of presence feels different. It's not silence rooted in punishment or insecurity. It's not pulling back to punish or pressure. It's simply a decision to stay rooted in your own rhythm, rather than chasing someone else's. In this space, you are not freezing or hiding. You are allowing. You are letting life come toward you, rather than forcing it to unfold on your terms.

The more attuned you become to your own body, the more easily you'll feel when this space is empowered and when it turns anxious. The body tells the truth. If you find yourself holding back words with tightness in your chest, clenching in your belly, or obsessive looping in your mind, it may not be space at all. It may be fear dressed as strategy. But if you feel a calm, grounded openness, even in the unknown, that is true space. That's where the chase becomes magnetic.

This kind of space asks you to trust the masculine's ability to move. Not because he will always do it perfectly, but because you are no longer trying to carry both poles. You are no longer trying to be the initiator, the emotional container, and the seductress all at once. You are giving yourself permission to rest in your feminine, to be witnessed and responded to without always making the first move.

This does not mean you suppress your desires or dim your voice. On the contrary, feminine space is honest. It speaks clearly when something matters. It sets boundaries when something is off. But it does so without urgency. Without clinging. Without needing the other person to validate its worth. This is the difference between self-honoring expression and emotional leakage. One comes from fullness, the other from fear.

When you learn to sit in this space, you start to see the dance more clearly. You notice when someone approaches from true desire rather than obligation. You recognize who is drawn to your frequency versus who is trying to fix or possess it. This clarity only arises when you stop overreaching. When you stop chasing people for answers they cannot give you.

In this way, space becomes a tool for energetic discernment. You don't have to test people or create artificial distance. You simply honor your own energy enough to let it move at its natural pace. This often means allowing silence between texts, letting invitations come without prompting them, and not filling every void with explanation. It means feeling the urge to reach out and choosing, just for a moment, to stay with yourself instead.

Not because you're playing a role. But because you're beginning to realize that the more you source your power internally, the less you need to grasp for it externally. The less you rush to be chosen, the more you become irresistible. The less you collapse into others' timelines, the more they begin to move toward yours.

There is a kind of beauty that arises in the space you create when you stop trying to control the outcome. It's the beauty of allowing another to arrive in their own time. It's the beauty of letting yourself be seen without performing. It's the grace of trusting that what's real does not need to be forced.

You are not an algorithm to be solved. You are not a puzzle to be unlocked. You are a woman in her fullness. The kind of woman who knows how to create space without turning cold, who knows how to invite without chasing, who knows that her presence alone can ignite pursuit. Not because she withholds love, but because she holds it so completely that it cannot be taken, only met.

This is not manipulation. This is power. Sacred, grounded, feminine power. And it never begs to be chased. It simply allows itself to be found.

Part III. The Psychology of Seduction & Influence

Seduction is often misunderstood. It's mistaken for manipulation, for games, for something shallow or performative. But in truth, real seduction is energetic. It's psychological. It's the art of creating space where connection, desire, and devotion can unfold naturally. It has nothing to do with forcing someone to feel something they don't, and everything to do with amplifying what's already there beneath the surface.

This part of the journey is about understanding what moves people at their core—not just what they want, but what drives them to act, to pursue, to choose. Influence, when aligned with integrity, is not about control. It's about resonance. And feminine influence is one of the most powerful forces on earth, because it bypasses logic and speaks directly to the emotional and energetic center.

You've already begun to embody your feminine energy. You've started anchoring into your body, deepening your magnetic field, and practicing how to hold space without collapsing. Now, you're ready to understand the invisible mechanics behind what draws people in, keeps them captivated, and builds true connection without chasing.

This part of the book will not give you tricks. It will give you power. The kind of power that is quiet, but undeniable. The kind of presence that doesn't need to perform, yet shifts the entire atmosphere of a room. Because it's not just about how you look, speak, or walk—it's about how you **are**. And how that state of being affects those around you.

Every person is unconsciously scanning for cues. Cues of safety. Of confidence. Of allure. Most of this happens below the threshold of conscious awareness. But when you understand how these signals work— how people interpret tone, space, timing, vulnerability, and confidence— you stop feeling at the mercy of others' attention, and start becoming the one they orient around.

85

This is where we explore polarity from a psychological angle. Where you learn how the masculine mind perceives energy, presence, and emotional charge. Where you stop fearing influence and start honoring your capacity to lead with presence, not pressure. Because real seduction doesn't override someone's will. It awakens it.

We'll explore how mystery isn't about hiding, but about being fully seen in layers. How the most magnetic women are not always the loudest or boldest, but the most emotionally attuned. And how you can begin using your words, your timing, your distance, and your embodiment to create a gravitational pull that is not just felt, but remembered.

Seduction is not a mask. It's a deep unveiling. The feminine doesn't need to manipulate to get attention. She needs to remember who she is, so she can **influence without effort**. And when you approach it from this place, you no longer fear the game—because you're not playing it. You're mastering the energy that makes others come closer on their own.

This part of the book will show you how to use that energy with respect, clarity, and confidence. Not to get someone to validate you. But to step fully into your power and let the world respond to the truth of your presence.

Chapter 7: Seduction Is an Energy, Not a Script

Why Seduction Is Not About Sex (But About Power)

Seduction, in its truest form, is not about sex. It is about power. Not dominance. Not force. But the power to shift energy, awaken desire, and magnetize attention without chasing. This kind of power lives deep within the feminine. It's not loud, performative, or dramatic. It doesn't scream for validation. It moves subtly, but undeniably. And once it's activated, it doesn't need to ask for permission to be felt.

We've been conditioned to reduce seduction to physicality. To skin. To lingerie. To angles and aesthetics. We've been sold the image of seduction as something sexualized, where its worth is measured by how much someone else wants your body. But true seduction isn't about being desired. It's about how you hold yourself while being seen. How you move through the world with such embodied confidence that people can't look away—not because of your body, but because of your presence.

Sex may be one expression of seduction. But it's only a small part. The deeper layers of seduction lie in energy. In the pause before you speak. In the way you let silence linger. In how you look at someone without urgency, without grasping. Real seduction is the absence of neediness. It is the art of holding space so powerfully that others feel pulled toward you and want to stay there.

Because what actually pulls someone in is not your body, but your emotional gravity. People are drawn to women who know who they are. Who aren't trying to perform or prove. Who aren't leaking energy to get attention. There is power in restraint. In stillness. In choosing not to fill every moment with words, explanations, or apologies. The feminine seductress understands this. She doesn't manipulate. She simply embodies her own worth so deeply that others start adjusting themselves to meet her where she already is.

This is why seduction is not a skill you perform, but a state you embody. It's not about doing something to get a reaction. It's about living in a way that naturally produces attraction. And when this power is fully rooted, it affects how others feel in your presence. They lean in. They soften. They want more—not because you gave them something, but because your energy itself is a transmission of confidence, sensuality, and sovereignty.

You don't have to flirt to be seductive. You don't have to speak a certain way or dress a certain way. You don't even have to talk about sex. You only need to learn how to become so energetically full, so turned on by your own presence and power, that others can't help but feel it. This isn't something you fake. It's something you practice and embody until it becomes your natural frequency.

And that is the real secret: seduction is not about technique. It's about frequency. Some women are magnetic without saying a word. Others say all the right things but leave no impact. The difference lies in whether the energy is coming from a place of lack or a place of abundance. A woman who knows her worth doesn't seduce to be validated. She seduces by simply being fully herself—and letting others respond how they will.

You're not here to convince anyone. You're here to remember that your power isn't something you earn. It's something you access. And once you begin accessing it, seduction stops being something you try to do. It becomes something you naturally are.

That kind of embodied magnetism doesn't come from studying seduction tactics. It comes from living in alignment with your own truth, claiming your emotions without shame, and allowing your sensuality to be a natural extension of your self-awareness. When you are deeply anchored in your body, when you are not trying to be impressive but simply present, your field becomes irresistible. Not because you are pleasing, but because you are powerful.

Many women unconsciously use seduction as a survival strategy. They adapt themselves to be liked, to be wanted, to be chosen. They shift their tone, suppress their needs, and read the room constantly to gauge how much of themselves they can safely reveal. This is not seduction. This is self-abandonment in disguise. And it's draining. It keeps you in a loop of performance where your worth is measured by external reaction.

Powerful seduction doesn't require you to diminish yourself for approval. It asks you to deepen into who you already are. It invites you to hold your center when attention comes and when it doesn't. To become so energetically sovereign that you don't seek a response, but remain rooted in your own presence, letting others orbit you rather than collapsing into them. That presence is magnetic because it holds contrast. There is softness and sharpness. There is mystery and clarity. There is availability without urgency. You don't need to be constantly accessible. You don't need to explain your boundaries or justify your preferences. Your body language, your energy, your stillness all speak on your behalf. And what they communicate is: I am not here to chase, to perform, or to seduce you into loving me. I am here to be fully in myself, and that alone is enough.

This depth of power is what most people are truly longing for. Even if they can't articulate it, they feel the difference. One woman might trigger attraction with her body, but another awakens something deeper simply by the way she listens, breathes, and takes up space without apology. One is momentary. The other is unforgettable.

That's why this kind of seduction isn't about being noticed. It's about being felt. You stop trying to charm. You stop trying to perfect. You stop needing to manage perception. Instead, you move with the confidence of someone who knows her energy has its own intelligence. You know your presence is enough to shift the dynamic in a room without raising your voice or showing more skin.

From this place, seduction becomes sacred. It becomes a form of energetic leadership, not a game to win. It's a reclamation of your feminine depth, your erotic current, your emotional truth. It teaches you to stay fully alive in your own skin, even when no one is watching. Because that's where the real power is—in how you hold yourself when there is nothing to prove and no one to please.

Let your body be the instrument, not the bait. Let your words land because they are true, not because they are rehearsed. Let your energy lead. Because when you stop trying to seduce, and start embodying your essence fully, you become the very thing others are unconsciously searching for.

And that is the most potent seduction of all.

The Invisible Language of Feminine Influence

There is a language that speaks louder than words, yet cannot be heard. A current that weaves through glances, pauses, movements, and the unspoken presence you bring into a space. It does not rely on logic or persuasion. It does not argue, prove, or demand. And yet it shifts dynamics, draws attention, and alters behavior. This is the invisible language of feminine influence.

Unlike the masculine mode of influence, which often moves through direction, assertion, or structured frameworks, feminine influence is relational. It is not linear. It flows through nuance, through energy, through presence. It isn't about making someone do something. It's about subtly altering the emotional field until what you desire becomes the most natural response. Not through force, but through felt resonance.

Your nervous system plays a central role in this. When you are regulated, grounded, and connected to yourself, others instinctively tune to your frequency. They feel safe. They feel drawn. This is not about being soft for the sake of pleasing. It's about stability. When a woman walks into a room with deep coherence in her energy, without inner conflict or noise, people notice. Even if she says nothing. Even if she barely moves. Her influence isn't performative. It's embodied.

This silent power isn't loud, but it is unforgettable. It speaks through the way you hold your gaze without chasing. Through the way you take a breath before responding, creating space rather than reaction. Through the way you move—fluidly, unapologetically, without rushing to meet anyone else's pace.

Most women have been taught that influence comes from perfecting the external. The right tone, the right outfit, the right words. But the deeper truth is that real feminine influence begins in the unseen. It begins in the field you carry. In your ability to listen with your whole body. In the subtle opening of your posture, the quality of stillness in your presence, the warmth or coolness of your attention.

There is a difference between trying to get someone to feel something and simply becoming the invitation for that feeling. The former is manipulation, often rooted in insecurity. The latter is magnetism, born from depth and self-trust. Influence that lasts does not come from control, but from clarity.

Clarity of who you are, what you allow, and what you no longer need to explain.

The invisible language also operates through polarity. The more anchored you are in your feminine, the more you awaken the masculine in others—not by effort, but by contrast. You don't have to "do" more to influence. You often have to do less. Soften. Slow down. Let your presence expand instead of collapsing into action. Let your receptivity create the space where others step forward.

This is not weakness. It's refinement. It's knowing that the most powerful energy is often the one that doesn't push, but pulls. That influence is not about being at the center of attention, but about holding the center of gravity.

Let's now go deeper into what this looks like in motion. How it expresses through your body, your voice, your silence. And how to become fluent in this language—not by learning it from the outside, but by remembering it from within.

The body is where this language becomes fluent. Every step you take, every tilt of the head, every pause in conversation transmits something deeper than words ever could. The nervous system of the person across from you picks up on your cues before their mind even understands what's happening. That's how influence begins—not through content, but through state. Your felt state is your transmission.

If you walk into a room holding tension in your jaw, with your breath stuck high in your chest, the energy you emit is guarded. If you walk in with softened shoulders, a grounded belly, and your awareness rooted in the lower half of your body, your presence speaks of ease, availability, and quiet strength. That presence makes people lean in, without knowing why.

This doesn't mean walking slowly or trying to appear graceful. It means inhabiting your body in a way that makes you feel deeply connected to yourself. When your awareness fills your body, others feel it. There is no need for performance. The feminine does not influence by being louder. She influences by being more present.

Your voice is another channel. Not just the words you use, but the quality behind them. A voice that carries softness, space, and clarity often cuts through noise more effectively than a raised tone or sharp words. This doesn't mean making your voice smaller. It means letting your voice come from a place that's fully embodied, resonant, and not seeking approval.

Even silence, when embodied, is magnetic. Not the silence that comes from suppression or fear, but the kind that holds energy, curiosity, and power. When you are not in a rush to fill every gap, you create an atmosphere where others reveal themselves more. Influence happens not because you dominated the space, but because you created the conditions for something deeper to emerge.

This is where so many women get trapped—thinking they must perform, perfect, or prove. But the real art is in revealing rather than performing. You reveal your essence by being so deeply rooted in your own body, your own truth, that you no longer adjust for others. You become the tuning fork. You invite others to come into resonance with you.

The invisible language of feminine influence requires inner attunement before external impact. You must become aware of the subtle ways you contract when you don't feel safe, or the ways you overextend to avoid discomfort. Influence does not come from bypassing these moments, but from noticing them, breathing into them, and choosing a new way of being. That moment of shift is the moment of power.

There is nothing manipulative about this. It is not about playing games or creating illusions. It is about deep honesty with yourself. When you shift internally, everything around you shifts. The way people listen, respond, engage—it all mirrors your energetic stance.

Influence, when rooted in embodiment, becomes a form of leadership. Not through force, but through coherence. Not through domination, but through depth. The most influential women are often not the most aggressive or visible, but the most grounded, the most integrated. They move differently. They respond instead of react. They create space where others feel seen, yet challenged. Held, yet awakened.

And the most powerful truth of all is this: the invisible language cannot be faked. It must be lived. When you embody what you say, you don't need to say much at all. When you embody your own magnetism, you don't need to chase anything. You already are the gravity.

Using Mystery, Slowness, and Polarity to Become Irresistible

There is a kind of presence that makes people stop and feel something without knowing why. It's not about being the most beautiful in the room, or the loudest, or the most talked about. It's the woman who carries herself with a subtle charge, who leaves spaces in her energy, who doesn't rush to fill silence, and who feels deeply but reveals slowly. That presence is born of mystery, slowness, and polarity. And it's magnetic.

Mystery is not the act of hiding. It is the art of revealing only what is aligned, only when it serves, only from a place of rooted power. The moment you try to create mystery to manipulate someone's curiosity, it becomes performance. But when you are genuinely connected to your own depth—when you are living with your own questions, exploring your own edges—you don't need to force mystery. You become it.

So many women, in an effort to be understood or validated, over-explain themselves. They pour everything out, hoping that more transparency will equal more closeness. But that kind of unfiltered exposure often dissolves attraction. When everything is out on the table too soon, there's nothing left to feel into, no tension to hold, no discovery to be made.

A woman who is connected to her own mystery is not withholding. She's simply not leaking. She knows the power of being fully present without being fully available. She listens without rushing to respond. She moves without needing to be noticed. She speaks only when it comes from something real. This doesn't make her cold or inaccessible. It makes her irresistible.

Slowness amplifies this effect. In a culture obsessed with speed and productivity, slowness feels rebellious. It invites the nervous system to soften. It makes room for nuance, for subtlety, for awareness. Most people move quickly because they're not fully present. They're chasing the next thing. But the woman who walks slowly, speaks slowly, breathes deeply—she moves with intent. She holds the room without effort.

Slowness is not laziness. It's power. It signals that you are not chasing, not proving, not desperate to be chosen. When you slow down, you give others a chance to feel you. You give yourself a chance to listen to your own cues. You stop moving from reaction, and start moving from resonance.

Polarity is what makes the dynamic electric. It's the tension between opposites that fuels desire and influence. Feminine energy is the receptive, intuitive, magnetic current. Masculine energy is the directive, structured, penetrative force. When a woman fully embodies her feminine polarity, she naturally creates a space that draws the masculine out. Not by demanding it, but by being the invitation to it.

This doesn't mean you must always stay in the feminine. It means becoming skillful in recognizing which energy is alive in you, and how it's being expressed. If you're always directing, controlling, leading, deciding, then you're holding masculine energy by default. There's nothing wrong with that—but it will neutralize the charge in certain dynamics, especially romantic or energetic ones. Polarity requires contrast. Not sameness.

Letting yourself lean back, receive, feel, and express from the body reawakens your feminine current. This current is not passive. It is wild, potent, creative, and chaotic in the most beautiful way. But it cannot be forced. It must be allowed.

What makes you irresistible is not that you try to be feminine. It's that you let yourself *be felt* in your feminine. That energy communicates through your eyes, your breath, the way you turn your head, the way you respond instead of react. When you're truly in that space, others feel a pull toward you that is not logical. It's magnetic. It's energetic. It's real.

You don't need to tell someone what you are. You only need to embody it. If you're trying to convince someone of your value, the energy underneath is lack. But when you inhabit your value fully, without pushing, it speaks through the texture of your presence. That's what makes people lean in. Not because you're trying to get them to, but because they feel something they want more of. Something rare. Something regulated and whole.

Mystery lives in the pauses. In the moments you don't rush to fill. In the eyes that linger just a second longer before looking away. It's in the absence of urgency, the refusal to overshare, the quiet confidence of a woman who is not asking to be figured out. Not because she's playing a role, but because she's actively exploring herself. That depth, that self-containment, makes everything she chooses to reveal carry weight.

Slowness doesn't just shift how others experience you. It rewires how you experience yourself. It breaks the momentum of reaction. When you walk slowly, you start to feel the texture of your body. When you speak slowly, you start to hear the truth in your voice. When you make love slowly, you start to feel your own hunger more clearly. This kind of embodiment is not for performance. It's for reclamation.

And polarity becomes the natural consequence of that reclamation. You don't need to study masculine and feminine energy in a textbook to feel it. You can sense it in your body. When you soften into your hips, into your breath, into your receptivity, something in the space shifts. Masculine energy either rises to meet you or reveals its inability to hold you. But you're not reaching. You're not fixing. You're not adjusting yourself to provoke it. You're rooted. That's where your power is.

The most magnetic women don't chase. They attract. Not through silence or passivity, but through alignment. Their mystery is not a mask. It's the echo of something sacred being protected. Their slowness is not hesitation. It's precision. Their polarity is not decoration. It's embodiment. They don't seduce to get something. They simply are. And that "being" is irresistible because it's rare.

In a world where most people are starving for depth and trying to fill the void with stimulation, you become unforgettable when you become a portal to something slower, deeper, more rooted in essence. You give others the experience of their own presence, simply by living in yours. That's influence. That's seduction. That's power.

It doesn't require performance or perfection. You don't need to always be graceful or say the perfect thing. In fact, rawness and authenticity will only deepen your magnetism when they're held in truth. You can cry and still be powerful. You can tremble and still be magnetic. What matters is whether your energy is *with you* or being thrown outward to be received.

Your feminine influence begins with self-connection. The more you allow yourself to feel, the more you activate your own current. The more you allow space in your expression, the more others want to step into it. This is not about being chased. It's about becoming the kind of woman who is not only desirable, but unforgettable. Because she doesn't grasp. She doesn't perform. She just *is*.

Mystery, slowness, and polarity are not tactics. They're portals into your own energetic truth. When you trust that truth, you no longer need to force attraction. You become the resonance that others didn't even know they were craving.

95

Chapter 8: Becoming the Frame, Not the Reaction

What It Means to 'Hold the Frame' Energetically

To hold the frame energetically means you become the silent structure that reality shapes itself around. It's not about controlling people, raising your voice, or asserting dominance in a loud or performative way. It's about becoming the unshakable center that does not collapse under external pressure, emotional chaos, or shifting dynamics. You don't adapt to the mood in the room. You *are* the mood in the room.

This isn't an intellectual stance. It's a felt sense in your body. A regulation of your nervous system so solid that others instinctively entrain to your energy. When you hold the frame, your presence communicates, "This is the standard. This is the rhythm. This is the temperature." And without you saying a word, others start responding to it. They slow down. They lean in. They adjust.

But it only works if it's real. If you're faking calm, people will sense it. If your energy is frantic underneath a still surface, they'll feel the dissonance. True frame holding requires embodiment. Not just confidence, but rootedness. Not just presence, but power that doesn't leak. It's the difference between someone who knows they're magnetic and someone trying to appear that way.

You can tell when someone has no frame. They constantly scan for cues. They shift themselves to keep peace, to seek approval, to stay liked. Their energy molds to the strongest presence in the room, even when it betrays their values. They lose themselves in connection, then wonder why they feel drained or disrespected.

Holding the frame isn't about walls. It's not cold or distant. It's warm, grounded containment. It's knowing what you will allow into your space, and what will not be permitted to disturb your peace. It's refusing to participate in dysfunction just because it's easier than holding boundaries. And it's the invisible force that makes others instinctively trust you, respect you, and magnetize to you.

In relationships, this is where true polarity lives. If you collapse every time someone withdraws, if you over-explain every decision, if your energy scrambles to accommodate theirs, the frame is gone. And when the frame is gone, attraction often follows. That doesn't mean you need to be rigid. But it does mean you must stay connected to your own core even when someone else's energy is pulling you off center.

This is especially true in dynamics where emotional intensity is high. When someone tests you, challenges you, or even tries to provoke you, the way you respond tells them everything. If your energy stays anchored, if your body doesn't tense, if your tone remains clean and firm, the test dissolves. Because they were never testing your logic. They were testing your center.

And to stay centered, you must be able to feel everything without becoming it. You must allow emotion to move through you without letting it dictate your direction. You must be able to be present with someone else's chaos without absorbing it or reacting to it. This is the art of containment. Not for them, but for yourself. So that your energy remains yours, even in intimacy.

True power lives here. Not in manipulation, not in control, but in unwavering alignment with your own truth. When you hold the frame, you stop seeking confirmation. You stop needing validation. You become the atmosphere people remember, even if they can't explain why.

People are drawn to those who hold their own frame because it offers a sense of safety. Not the safety of comfort or agreement, but the deeper safety of coherence. Your nervous system communicates, "I'm not going to disappear. I'm not going to crumble. You can rage, pull away, test me, even seduce me, and I will still be here in myself." That is rare. And that is what makes it irresistible.

Energetically, this requires precision. It's not just about standing firm, but about holding steady without freezing. The moment your frame becomes rigidity, it's no longer presence. It's armor. The body hardens. The energy locks. You're no longer available, just defended. A real frame is both rooted and responsive. It feels what's happening but isn't ruled by it.

The feminine, in particular, senses the difference between a man who is grounded in his own frame and one who is posturing. One creates polarity. The other breaks trust. And when polarity fades, so does the electricity. The same is true for the woman who embodies her own emotional center. She doesn't abandon herself to stay connected. She doesn't chase. She doesn't collapse into over-giving. She holds a field that invites pursuit, not through withholding, but through unwavering self-respect.

This isn't about detachment. It's about energetic leadership. And that leadership begins with self. You lead your own state. You lead your own reactions. You lead your own frequency. From that place, you don't have to force anyone to follow. They feel it. The magnetism happens on its own.

It's easy to lose the frame when the stakes feel high. When you care about someone. When you want the connection to last. But this is when holding the frame matters most. Because if you abandon it, you stop being who they were drawn to in the first place. You become the version of yourself that is willing to shrink to be loved. And deep down, you know they're not loving the real you.

You cannot hold the frame for both people in a relationship. You can only hold your own. If someone else is constantly testing or projecting or pulling you into their chaos, the work is not to stabilize them. The work is to see whether you're still rooted or whether you've been pulled out of yourself. If you have, you come back. If you haven't, you stay steady. Either way, you don't leave your own center to fix theirs.

This skill bleeds into every part of life. Business. Family. Social presence. The more you hold the frame, the more others sense your internal authority. Not the kind that needs to be obeyed, but the kind that others instinctively respect. Even in disagreement. Even in silence. Especially in silence. Because in a world full of noise and insecurity, your calm, clear presence becomes the rarest signal of all.

To develop this, you have to become deeply aware of your own energetic patterns. Where do you lose yourself? Where does your nervous system spike? What kind of energy makes you want to rush in and fix, or withdraw and protect? These are your gateways. Your training grounds. And each time you notice without reacting, you deepen your ability to stay in the seat of your own power.

It is not about dominance. It is not about control. It is about self-possession. Holding the frame energetically is the art of staying rooted, open, and sovereign, even when the world around you wobbles. That is the kind of power people feel but cannot name. That is what creates true influence. And that is what makes your presence unforgettable.

Training Others How to Respond to You Without a Word

You are always teaching people how to treat you. Whether you speak or stay silent, whether you lean forward or pull away, whether you soften or tense— your body tells a story. Your energy sets the rules of engagement long before your mouth does.

Most people think boundaries are verbal declarations. But before words ever form, boundaries already live in your posture, your gaze, your pace, and your presence. People feel them. They may not know why they hesitate before interrupting you, why they hold your gaze longer than they expected to, or why they suddenly find themselves matching your pace. But it's because they've already been trained by your field.

This is not about becoming intimidating. It's about becoming internally congruent. When your nervous system, body language, and emotional tone are aligned, you send out a clear signal. You don't have to raise your voice. You don't have to over-explain. You don't have to defend your value. You embody it. That silent transmission is far more effective than trying to convince anyone of who you are.

The key is awareness. If your words say one thing but your energy signals something else, people won't trust the surface. They'll respond to the undercurrent. You might say "I'm fine," but your subtle tension teaches them to tiptoe around you. You might say "I don't mind," but your nervous smile trains them to ignore your needs. The invitation here is not to perform better. It's to become more honest in your presence.

To train others to respond with respect, clarity, or care, you must hold those standards within your own energy first. Not by demanding them, but by living them. When you truly respect yourself, others feel the weight of it. When you are clear within, your silence carries more authority than someone else's noise. And when you are emotionally available without leaking or collapsing, your presence becomes a mirror. It reflects to others what is possible.

Most people respond not to who you are but to who you are being in the moment. If your energy is porous, they may overstep. If your field is contracted, they may pull away. But if your energy is rooted, open, and intentional, they will almost always attune without realizing it. This is not manipulation. This is resonance.

You don't have to perform dominance. You don't have to become louder or colder or tougher. In fact, those traits often signal the opposite of power. What commands attention is someone who is deeply at peace with their own presence. Someone who doesn't need validation to feel worthy. Someone who doesn't need to be feared to feel strong. When you hold that posture—soft but firm, open but anchored—you become someone others instinctively regulate themselves around.

The subtle training begins in the micro-moments. How you enter a room. How you hold eye contact. Whether your body collapses inward or rises with awareness. These are all cues that the nervous system picks up instantly. And once you begin sending them consistently, people stop testing your boundaries. Not because they were told, but because they feel where the line is. They sense that crossing it would disorganize the connection. So instead, they meet you where you already are.

When you are internally coherent, your boundaries are not a performance. They become an energetic fact. And this coherence doesn't come from overthinking every movement or trying to control perception. It comes from self-trust. From the slow, daily return to your own center. The more deeply you trust yourself, the less you fidget with your presentation. Your body relaxes, your face softens, and yet your presence grows unmistakably sharper. People feel that contrast. It calibrates them in real time.

At a nervous system level, others are constantly picking up signals from your subtle field. They notice the way you exhale before speaking. They track how still you remain when others are restless. They register the tension in your jaw when your needs are unmet, even if your mouth stays shut. That's why the work begins with you. If your system is dysregulated, your presence becomes either too open or too guarded. In both cases, others feel confused about how to engage with you. But when you've learned to ground your energy, emotions, and posture into alignment, you create safety without saying a word. That safety is what invites both respect and attraction.

This is especially potent in dynamics where words have been overused. Some people are trained to ignore verbal boundaries. Others are too skilled at masking their true intentions. But almost no one can resist the clarity of energy that is settled and deliberate. In the presence of that kind of signal, they either rise or retreat. And either outcome brings truth to the surface, without needing a single confrontation.

If you've ever walked into a room and felt someone's attention without seeing them move, you've already felt the power of silent influence. It is not about being loud. It is about being rooted. Someone who is energetically rooted does not chase. They do not fawn. They do not collapse or inflate. They hold. And by holding, they shift the climate of the space around them. What this requires is not emotional perfection, but clarity of signal. If you're upset, own it without bleeding it. If you're disappointed, let your eyes speak it without resentment. If you're done, let your silence hold more finality than a hundred explanations. That level of energetic precision is something people remember. It creates imprint. And imprints don't need repeating.

The mistake many make is trying to speak power into being. But real power does not announce itself. It is revealed through congruence. When your tone, timing, breath, and gaze all agree, people feel pulled to respect you, even if they don't understand why. They may say things like "there's just something about you" or "you have this presence" because they lack the language for what they're sensing. What they're really experiencing is the rare clarity of a person who doesn't leak their energy.

To embody this kind of clarity, begin by watching yourself in everyday moments. Notice where you abandon your center to smooth over a conversation. Feel the difference between walking into a room with presence versus entering with apology. Pay attention to what your body does when someone disrespects you—does it freeze, lean forward, or contract? These are not flaws. They are signals. And when you see them, you can choose to rewire the response. Not with force. But with breath. With posture. With intention.

Eventually, you'll find that you don't need to ask for better treatment. Your field becomes the request. And the people who are attuned to power, not control, will meet it with reverence. Not out of obligation. But because you've already trained them to recognize what you will and will not hold, without ever raising your voice.

Subtle Influence Tactics for Everyday Power Plays

Power plays don't always happen in high-stakes environments. Most of them unfold in daily moments: a glance held too long, a favor asked without context, a pause before replying. Influence is not always about controlling others. In its feminine expression, it is about guiding the emotional current without ever needing to swim upstream. It's the quiet redirection of energy that happens through your presence, your timing, and the subtle way you respond to invisible cues others miss.

In everyday interactions, people are constantly scanning for who holds the frame. The frame is the unspoken structure of the moment: whose pace are we following, whose emotional tone is leading, whose needs are being centered. You can walk into a conversation already shaped by someone else's mood, or you can learn to reshape the field simply by shifting your own internal state. This doesn't require force or performance. It begins with awareness.

The first and most powerful tactic of subtle influence is stillness. In a world addicted to overexplaining and reacting, stillness creates gravity. When someone makes a subtle jab or a manipulative comment, most people instinctively respond with defense or deflection. But stillness, especially paired with a soft gaze or a delayed response, disrupts the power dynamic entirely. You become unreadable, and in doing so, you take the lead. The other person is left to sit in the energy they just created, unsure if it landed or backfired. This moment of uncertainty tilts the balance in your favor without you needing to lift a finger.

Another form of subtle influence lies in selective attention. Where you place your gaze, your energy, your responsiveness — all of it teaches others what is important to you, what earns your presence, and what doesn't. When you reward manipulation with attention, you train people to use it. But when you withdraw your full presence the moment someone crosses a line or shifts into a low vibration, they feel the absence more than any reprimand. Over time, your silence becomes instruction. Your absence becomes correction.

There is also immense power in intentional timing. Most people rush to fill silence or reply immediately, trying to keep connection alive. But influence thrives in the space between stimulus and response. A pause before speaking creates anticipation. Waiting to respond to a message — not out of game-playing, but because you are actually grounded in your own rhythm — sends the signal that you are not energetically available on demand. You are pacing the exchange, not chasing it. And that pacing changes everything. People begin to adapt to your tempo. They become more intentional with their words. They lean in to seek your cues rather than trying to overpower them. This shift doesn't require you to be the loudest or the most dominant. It simply requires you to be anchored.

Nowhere is this more evident than in group settings. In a room full of voices, the one who speaks last — not because she waited passively, but because she observed actively — often ends up setting the tone. Her words carry more weight, not because they are louder, but because they are deliberate. When you speak with that level of care, people remember not just what you said, but how you made the room feel when you said it.

Influence, at its core, is not about strategy as much as it is about coherence. The more your words, your energy, and your presence are in alignment, the more impact you have with fewer moves. The game becomes subtle because you are no longer trying to win. You are simply radiating clarity, and that clarity begins to reorganize the dynamics around you.

Clarity is magnetic, not because it demands attention, but because it clears space for others to respond. Most people operate in a fog of self-doubt, seeking reactions, chasing validation, or second-guessing their place in the social current. When you stop doing that, when you become the one who moves with precision and inner certainty, the entire relational field bends toward you.

This is where another potent form of influence comes alive: energy containment. It's the ability to hold your emotional state without leaking it. You can be disappointed without becoming reactive. You can be intrigued without gushing. You can be interested without signaling need. This containment isn't about hiding your emotions or being inauthentic. It's about self-possession. You let others feel your presence without giving away your internal process. That restraint creates mystery. Mystery activates curiosity. And curiosity, when directed toward a grounded woman, becomes a channel for influence.

In moments of tension or conflict, this containment becomes even more powerful. The ability to not escalate, to not collapse, and to not rush to rescue the moment gives you full leverage. While others scramble to soothe, fix, or dominate, you sit back and observe. That observational power is underestimated. It allows you to notice patterns others miss. And when you do speak, you speak from clarity, not reaction. That difference is felt. You are no longer caught in the game — you are shaping it from the inside out. There's also an element of calibration that deepens your influence. You learn to adjust the intensity of your presence based on the energy of the room. Sometimes, subtle dominance is expressed by withholding. Other times, it's revealed through warmth and generosity. The key is to be conscious. Influence is not about applying the same posture everywhere. It's about sensing where the power is being misplaced or misused, and quietly shifting it without confrontation. That might mean changing your tone, holding eye contact longer than usual, or softening your voice to invite rather than overpower. It's a dance, not a script.

And yet, none of these tactics work unless you are rooted in self-respect. You must believe, deeply and consistently, that you are worthy of being listened to, honored, and followed. That belief doesn't have to be loud. In fact, it's often strongest in silence. It's the kind of inner conviction that radiates through body language, through the way you sit, the way you walk, the way you choose when and how to engage. Others feel it. They register it before you ever open your mouth.

The beauty of subtle influence is that it doesn't erode your integrity. You are not manipulating anyone. You are simply becoming more aware of how energy moves through space, and how you can direct it through intention and presence rather than force or performance. This kind of influence creates spaciousness in relationships. People feel more seen, more attuned, more naturally drawn toward alignment when they are around you. That's not because you push. It's because you hold your center so well that others recalibrate around you.

What makes this powerful is not how often you use it, but how precisely. Influence is not about constant effort. It's about well-placed pauses, well-timed responses, and the courage to let silence speak when words would only dilute your power. It's about letting your energy communicate what your mouth never has to say.

In a world obsessed with visibility, the true art lies in the unseen. The woman who masters subtle influence doesn't seek the spotlight. She creates gravity. And those around her, without even knowing why, start to orbit.

Chapter 9: Emotional Alchemy and High-Value Boundaries

Alchemizing Rage, Jealousy, and Insecurity Into Fuel

There are emotions we're told to hide. Emotions that are labeled as too much, too dark, too unseemly for a woman to feel — let alone express. Rage. Jealousy. Insecurity. The world calls them ugly. Dangerous. Undesirable. And yet, beneath the surface of every one of these states lies something potent. Something raw. Something that, if channeled with precision and presence, becomes fuel.

The feminine is not inherently soft. It is not always gentle or docile. True feminine energy holds multitudes. It can destroy, create, protect, and seduce. It can grieve deeply and burn fiercely. To embody the full spectrum of your feminine power, you cannot bypass the emotions you've been taught to suppress. You have to go into them. But not to become them — to *transmute* them.

Rage, at its core, is a boundary that was crossed. It signals violation. It tells you that something sacred was ignored, overlooked, or taken without your consent. When you suppress rage, it turns inward as self-hatred or spills outward as projection. But when you meet rage with stillness and breath, when you listen to what it is protecting, you begin to uncover the root. Rage often masks pain, abandonment, or betrayal. Yet once it is seen, its heat can become clarity. It sharpens your discernment. It reveals your standards. And when integrated, it births a kind of authority that does not need to shout.

Jealousy, on the surface, feels like comparison. Like lack. Like the gnawing feeling that someone else has what you don't. But at its root, jealousy is a signal of desire. It points to something in another that you long to awaken in yourself. That desire is sacred. The discomfort of jealousy is not a flaw, but a mirror. What if instead of resenting the woman who seems magnetic, sensual, or powerful, you asked yourself: what part of me is craving expression? What part of me wants to stop hiding?

When you alchemize jealousy, you do not compete. You awaken. You use the trigger as an invitation into embodiment. The woman you envy isn't

105

your enemy — she's your permission slip. And when you see her as that, her power no longer threatens you. It reflects you.

Insecurity, perhaps more than any other feeling, has been weaponized against women. It's been treated like a weakness. But insecurity is not a lack of worth — it's a disconnection from it. You were not born insecure. You learned to doubt yourself through the accumulation of unmet needs, silent wounds, and distorted reflections from the world around you. To transmute insecurity is not to pretend it's not there. It's to sit with the parts of yourself that feel unworthy, and meet them with unshakable presence.

You do not need to be flawless to be powerful. You need to be integrated. The more you own your insecurities without performing confidence, the more grounded your power becomes. It's not about becoming someone else. It's about removing the noise between you and the truth of who you already are.

Every time you feel that surge of rage in your chest, that ache of jealousy in your belly, or that shrinking sense of doubt in your heart, you are being handed an invitation. The energy of these emotions is *not* the problem. It is the unused fuel of your evolution.

To engage with these emotions consciously, you must stop trying to be "above" them. You don't need to be more evolved than your rage, more graceful than your jealousy, or more secure than your insecurity. What you need is intimacy with your own emotional currents. You need to feel what you feel all the way through, without collapsing into it or trying to fix it. This is how you stop reacting, and start responding.

The power lies in presence. Rage becomes destructive when it's rushed or denied. But when held with fierce clarity, it teaches you where your values are, where your energy is being drained, and what must no longer be tolerated. Let it move through the body. Let it scream in your journal. Let it rise without needing to be acted upon. You're not losing control. You're learning how to reclaim it.

Jealousy, too, becomes sacred when you stop attaching shame to it. Trace it to its source. What do you think she has that you don't? What would you feel if you had that same magnetism, beauty, or power? Would you feel safer? More free? More wanted? That is not about her. That's a message from your own desire system. And that desire is pointing you toward a part of yourself you haven't allowed to fully breathe. Channel that energy into your embodiment. Feed it into your rituals. Let it push you into deeper intimacy with your own expression.

And insecurity, when softened into, will often reveal a younger part of you that was left behind. The version of you that didn't get to feel chosen, protected, validated, or seen. She's not a liability. She's the root of your rawest truth. When you ignore her, she hijacks your confidence. But when you see her, tend to her, and speak to her with warmth and power, you begin to rewire the internal relationship that forms the foundation of all outer ones. Insecurity begins to fade not because you've masked it, but because you've made peace with the voice behind it.

None of this happens in the mind alone. Alchemy is not a mental process. It is felt. It is physical. These energies move through the body before they ever take form in your words or actions. So you need to return to the body. Movement, breath, sound, stillness. Let your body express what your voice hasn't. Let your body cry, tremble, stretch, roar, or pulse with whatever truth has been buried. This is not emotional indulgence. This is emotional sovereignty.

When you meet your darkest feelings with reverence rather than resistance, they stop ruling you in secret. They start serving you with precision. Rage sharpens your edges. Jealousy reclaims your desire. Insecurity grounds your softness. You become a woman who is no longer shaped by her wounds, but sculpted by her ability to transmute them.

This is what makes you magnetic. Not surface confidence. Not pretending nothing gets to you. But the depth you carry when you've walked into your own fire and learned how to dance with it. The woman who has turned pain into power does not need to prove anything. Her energy speaks before her words do. She is not perfect, but she is potent.

And that potency? It doesn't come from being untouched by darkness. It comes from knowing exactly how to turn that darkness into gold.

Creating Boundaries That Enchant, Not Repel

There is a difference between a wall and a boundary, and the feminine understands that difference in her bones. A wall is built from fear, from protection, from the expectation of harm. It says, "Stay away." A boundary, when rooted in embodied self-worth, whispers something entirely different. It says, "This is how to love me."

For the awakened feminine, boundaries are not punishments. They are invitations. They are not ultimatums, but spells—guidelines that teach others how to experience you, how to honor your rhythm, how to remain in your world without disrupting the energetic garden you've cultivated. And because your presence holds value, the rules for entering that presence must be clear. Not harsh. Not cold. But unmistakably felt.

When boundaries are born from anxiety, they repel. They come out sharp, brittle, or overly rehearsed. They are used as shields rather than anchors. But when they arise from inner sovereignty, they enchant. Because they are not about control. They are about clarity. And clarity, in the feminine, is magnetic.

This is why it matters less what you say and more how you hold yourself when you say it. You don't need to announce your worth with tension in your voice. You only need to let your frequency carry it. The woman who is fully landed in her own value does not over-explain her "no." She doesn't fear being misunderstood. She knows that her boundaries are not a disruption of connection. They are a refinement of it.

Enchanting boundaries are an art form. They are less about saying "don't do this" and more about saying "this is how I stay open to you." It's a subtle redirection. You are not freezing someone out. You are tuning the energy between you. You are creating a dynamic where your needs do not shrink the moment you feel attraction, or dissolve under pressure, or wait for approval to exist.

This is especially vital in feminine-masculine dynamics. The feminine may long to soften, to be held, to melt. But she cannot melt into someone who collapses her edges. Her boundaries are what allow her to open without losing herself. The masculine is drawn to a woman who is soft, yes—but also self-contained. Who doesn't leak energy trying to keep him close. Who doesn't bargain for breadcrumbs with a flexible sense of self. The masculine relaxes not around the woman who bends, but around the woman who holds her shape.

And here's the nuance: your boundary is not a rejection of him. It is a reflection of your relationship with yourself. You are not setting it to manipulate or punish. You are setting it because you trust your body's signals, your inner truth, and the sacredness of your own energy. And when you set it from that place, it invites him into a more conscious polarity. It signals that your energy cannot be earned through pressure, but through resonance.

The shift occurs when you stop performing boundaries and begin embodying them. When they are not lines you draw once you're already triggered, but energies you carry in your field before words are even spoken. You don't need to argue your worth. You don't need to rehearse a perfect script. You only need to stay rooted. Grounded in what your body knows. Unwavering in what your heart is available for. And calm in the face of anything that does not align with that.

Your calm is the enchantment.

When you can remain calm while holding your boundary, it disarms resistance. It disrupts old patterns, especially in those who are used to manipulation, guilt, or emotional outbursts as tools for control. Your grounded energy communicates that the boundary is not about fear or punishment. It is simply the natural rhythm of a woman who knows how she wants to be met.

This level of embodiment does something powerful: it teaches others how to attune. Without needing to correct them, without needing to justify or defend, your field begins to educate. Not through lectures, but through presence. Not through tension, but through alignment. Those who cannot or will not meet that frequency will naturally fall away. Those who can will rise. Not because you demanded it, but because your energy required it.

The real magic is that you don't lose love when you hold a boundary with softness. You lose illusions. Illusions about who someone is, about how much you needed their approval, about how far you were willing to bend to be chosen. What remains is clarity. And from clarity, intimacy can deepen— not just with others, but with yourself.

Boundaries, then, become a way of keeping your inner world clean. Like a sacred temple, your energy needs space to breathe, to create, to flourish. If you allow everyone to enter it without discernment, it becomes cluttered. No one wants to rest in a temple filled with noise. Your peace, your sensuality, your depth—they all thrive in spaces where only aligned energies are permitted to linger.

This is not about elitism. It's about energetic stewardship. Just like your body filters what it consumes, your field must filter what it allows in. If someone cannot respect your limits, it says more about their disconnection than about your boundaries. And when you try to compensate for that by softening your standards, you begin the slow erosion of your own magnetism.

It's tempting to believe that being more flexible or agreeable will make you more desirable. But magnetism doesn't live in the woman who pleases. It lives in the woman who honors her truth even when it's inconvenient. Even when she risks being misunderstood. Even when her "no" creates silence where there used to be attention. Because she knows that peace is more nourishing than proximity, and that being seen is better than being tolerated. Your boundaries are a mirror. They show you where you're still tempted to abandon yourself in the name of connection. They reveal the moments when you're willing to silence your own discomfort to keep the peace. But a boundary doesn't disturb peace. It creates it. Not always on the surface, but in the deeper layers of your being.

Sometimes, holding your boundary will shake the ground beneath a relationship. And that's okay. Let it shake. Let it reveal what was never solid. What survives that shaking is what's real. What emerges on the other side is a new texture of connection—one where your truth has space, where your softness isn't taken for granted, and where your presence doesn't come at the cost of your power.

When you enchant with your boundaries, you aren't creating distance. You are creating precision. You are guiding energy with intention, refining the field around you, and letting every interaction become a reflection of your self-respect. This is not about being unapproachable. It's about being unmistakably clear.

In this clarity, you become unforgettable. Because most people don't encounter it often. They meet people who tolerate, bend, perform, and suppress. But when they meet you—anchored, calm, and unapologetic—

they remember. Not because you demanded attention, but because you became a standard.

And in that, the true feminine boundary becomes what it was always meant to be: not a wall, but a spell. A quiet enchantment that says, "If you want to be close to me, learn to move with care."

Using "No" as a Sacred Act of Power

There is a moment—quiet but potent—when a woman says "no" and everything shifts. Not because her voice was loud, or her tone was aggressive, but because the "no" came from a place that was anchored, sovereign, and unshakable. That "no" is not rejection. It is revelation. It reveals the line between self-abandonment and self-respect. It shows where her energy begins and where someone else's ends. It reminds the world that she is not here to be consumed, but to be met with reverence.

For many women, saying no has been tangled with fear: fear of being disliked, of being punished, of being labeled cold, rude, or selfish. So the "no" gets swallowed. Smoothed over. Hidden behind polite discomfort. And yet, each time it's avoided, something is quietly traded—her energy for their comfort, her truth for their approval.

But a "no" spoken from power doesn't need to be sharp. It doesn't need to carry tension. It becomes sacred when it is clean, embodied, and unapologetic. When it's not about pushing someone away, but about honoring the space where your truth lives. There is no need to justify it. No need to perform emotional labor to ease someone else's reaction. You simply say it, and you let it be.

This level of integrity creates a ripple in your life. Because when you stop fearing the discomfort your no might bring, you start standing in something larger than your momentary feelings. You stand in self-leadership. You step into the role of the woman who doesn't beg to be respected—she teaches by example. And in doing so, she grants others permission to do the same.

The sacred "no" is not just about people or situations you reject. It's about the inner reclamation of your clarity. The refusal to dilute your energy to fit into what was never designed to nourish you. It's the moment you recognize that preservation is not resistance. It's wisdom. And wisdom is magnetic.

Saying no becomes a sacred act when it's grounded in presence. That means you are not reacting out of trauma or trying to control the outcome. You are simply stating your alignment. It might be a no to an invitation. A no to an interaction. A no to continuing a dynamic that drains you. But underneath, it's always a yes to yourself. A yes to your energy. A yes to your boundaries, your rhythm, and your integrity.

This practice requires internal regulation. It asks you to hold the sensations that arise when you speak your truth. The flutter in your chest. The heat of vulnerability. The silence that might follow. And instead of collapsing into those sensations, you breathe. You root deeper. You become the woman who doesn't run from her own authority.

And in time, that "no" becomes more than a boundary. It becomes a frequency. One that is felt before it is heard. People begin to sense where you stand. They feel the sacredness of your space. Not because you told them, but because your energy no longer apologizes for being sovereign.

This is where we stop negotiating our standards and start embodying them. Not with harshness. Not with rigidity. But with grace. Because grace is not about softening our power. It's about using it with precision. And there is nothing more graceful than a woman who knows she doesn't owe anyone access to her time, her body, or her attention.

What begins to unfold when your "no" is non-negotiable is an energetic shift in your relationships. People adjust. Those who once relied on your silence to bypass your boundaries will either rise to meet you or fall away. Both outcomes are clarifying. You stop entertaining dynamics that feed on your compliance, and you start attracting those who respect your discernment. It becomes clear that saying no doesn't reduce connection— it refines it.

Your no stops being an event and becomes a presence. It's not something you deliver as a performance. It simply lives in your field. And because of that, the people around you no longer need to be told twice. They feel where the edges are. They sense that your yes carries weight precisely because your no is real. You become trustworthy, not only to others but to yourself.

That internal trust is what builds true power. When you honor your own signals, when you resist the impulse to override your body's wisdom for politeness or people-pleasing, you are no longer betraying yourself to keep the peace. That inner congruence creates an aura that doesn't need explanation. Your energy begins to speak louder than your words ever could.

There is also a softness that grows inside this kind of power. Not fragility, but a quiet certainty. You no longer need to defend yourself or overexplain your reasons. You don't need the other person to understand. You simply know what's right for you, and you live accordingly. This is the kind of presence that doesn't control others but influences them. It sets a tone. It becomes a mirror that reflects what others may not yet have claimed within themselves.

This sacred "no" is not about withdrawal or coldness. In fact, it deepens intimacy. When you are clear on what is aligned for you, you create a safer space for others to show up honestly too. You model authenticity. You create relationships based not on transaction or obligation, but on mutual respect and resonance. And from that foundation, real magnetism emerges. You begin to move through the world with a different posture. Not stiff or guarded, but rooted. You become the woman who listens deeply to herself before responding to anything or anyone. You don't rush to fill silence. You don't chase validation. You let your inner yes or no rise from your core, and you allow that to guide your next step.

Eventually, the fear of being perceived as "too much" or "too difficult" fades. It gets replaced by a deeper knowing: that your energy is sacred, and not everyone is meant to have access to it. You no longer dilute your truth to fit into rooms where your fullness is not welcomed. You stop explaining your worth and start embodying it. And in doing so, you create a field of permission for others to do the same.

There is nothing more powerful than a woman who holds herself as sacred. Not in theory. Not as a concept. But in the micro-moments of life. The invitations declined. The silence held. The boundaries honored. The redirection of her energy toward what truly nourishes her. Every no becomes a line in the sand, not of limitation, but of devotion. Devotion to her path. Devotion to her peace. Devotion to the version of herself she refuses to abandon ever again.

This is what it means to use "no" as a sacred act of power. Not to shut the world out, but to stay open without being consumed. To remain soft without being penetrated by what does not belong. To be clear without being cruel. To walk with a voice that is not loud, but unshakably clear. A woman whose no is clean becomes a woman whose yes is magnetic. And from that place, everything begins to shift in her favor. Not because she chased power, but because she remembered she already was it.

Part IV. Manifestation Through Feminine Codes

Manifestation is often taught through formulas and step-by-step strategies. Visualize, affirm, act, receive. But for the awakened feminine, that path feels hollow. Not because it's wrong, but because it's missing the essence that makes creation truly magnetic: embodiment, presence, and frequency. This part of the journey is not about becoming a better manifester by pushing harder or thinking more positively. It's about remembering that you *already are* the source.

The feminine doesn't manifest by force. She doesn't chase, grasp, or script the universe into submission. She moves through energy, through sensation, through alignment with the unseen codes that shape reality beneath the surface. She attracts by becoming the energetic match for what she desires, not by performing rituals without connection. And most of all, she calls in what is aligned by becoming unavailable for what is not.

This is where everything changes.

When you start moving from feminine codes, manifestation stops being about acquiring and starts being about becoming. You're no longer waiting for the external to shift so you can feel powerful. You become the energetic root of what you want to experience, and the world begins to respond to *you*. This is the quiet magnetism you've always felt beneath the noise. The power you've sensed but maybe didn't know how to access. Until now.

This part of the path is not about doing more. It's about tuning your energy into deep coherence with your truth. It's about regulating your nervous system so it can hold more. It's about refining your emotional frequency, not suppressing it. And it's about allowing the quantum field to meet you where you are—not where you pretend to be.

The codes you're about to unlock will not just help you create what you want. They'll help you become the kind of woman who doesn't have to reach for it. The one who embodies the frequency of her desires so deeply, reality bends in her direction. Not as a performance. Not as manipulation. But as a natural extension of her state.

That is the feminine way. She doesn't push the river. She becomes the ocean. And from that place, everything flows to her.

Let's begin.

Chapter 10: Rewiring the Subconscious Feminine Way

Why Logic Blocks Your Magnetic Power

Logic is a tool. It's sharp, precise, useful when building systems or solving puzzles. But when it comes to feminine magnetism, logic can become a cage. Not because thinking is wrong, but because trying to *think your way into power* pulls you out of your body, out of your field, and into the narrow corridors of control.

Magnetism doesn't live in the mind. It lives in the frequency you hold. And the feminine frequency isn't linear. It's not about clear steps, predictable sequences, or airtight reasoning. It's intuitive. Rhythmic. Sensual. Messy. Alive. It operates in the space before language, in the feeling behind your words, in the energy you carry long before you speak.

When you lean too heavily on logic, you stop listening to what your body is already saying. You start doubting your inner knowing. You wait for evidence before allowing yourself to trust. You override your instincts in favor of what *makes sense*. And by doing so, you disconnect from the very source of your feminine power: your energy.

This isn't about demonizing logic. It has its place. But in the realm of magnetism, it often becomes a shield. A way to feel safe by narrowing the field of possibilities to only what your conscious mind can explain. And that's the paradox. Because true magnetism requires you to open wider, not shrink smaller. To feel more, not analyze harder. To be available to the mystery of how things can come together without your interference.

The most magnetic women aren't the most logical. They're the most *attuned*. They trust what they feel even when it doesn't add up. They follow the sensation in their belly, the whisper in their heart, the quiet pulse of "yes" that makes no sense to anyone else. They move in alignment with something deeper than thought, and that's what makes them unforgettable.

You've likely been taught to dismiss this kind of inner knowing. To value certainty over intuition. To explain your choices instead of owning them. To protect yourself from being "irrational" or "emotional" or "too much."

But none of those traits are flaws in the feminine. They're portals. When you stop treating your feelings like threats to your logic, they start becoming keys to your power.

Because your magnetic field is not created by what you know. It's created by what you *feel* and how fully you let that feeling shape your state. Logic tries to control the outcome. The feminine lets the frequency speak. That doesn't mean you float through life without structure. It means you build your structure *around* the truth of your energy, not in opposition to it.

When you cling to logic, you stay in negotiation with your power. You second-guess your standards. You try to explain your boundaries. You look for the "why" before honoring the "no." You wait to feel safe before you say what you mean. But magnetism doesn't wait. It radiates. It doesn't justify itself. It doesn't ask for approval.

Letting go of logic doesn't mean you become careless. It means you learn to feel again. To trust the shift in your breath. The pull in your chest. The fire in your belly. It means you let those sensations guide you toward alignment, even if your mind screams that it's not the "smart" thing to do. Because the feminine doesn't thrive on smart. She thrives on true.

The body holds truth long before the mind catches up. When a situation feels off, when a boundary is crossed, when a decision is right but terrifying, your nervous system registers it before you have language for it. Your magnetism is sharpened in those moments where you choose to honor that subtle message rather than override it with reason.

The world will reward logic with safety, with predictability, with acceptance. But what it rarely rewards is deep feminine power. That is something you claim, not something you're given. And to claim it, you have to be willing to walk away from the rules of linear thinking and into the waters of your own feeling. You have to risk seeming irrational in a world obsessed with logic. You have to learn to live from your own inner rhythm, not the mental checklist of what's considered correct.

Many women numb themselves through overthinking. Not intentionally, but as a form of self-protection. They plan, analyze, anticipate, explain. They seek out frameworks, step-by-step systems, and proven strategies because it feels safer than feeling. But in doing so, they disconnect from the very intelligence that would have shown them the faster, more aligned path. The truth is, when you trust your energy, you move quicker and with more precision than any logical system could design.

Magnetism is clarity without needing to explain. It's the quiet certainty that doesn't beg to be understood. It's a woman who knows what she wants, not because she's made a pros and cons list, but because her entire being is in resonance with that desire. Her body lights up. Her breath deepens. She doesn't need to check if it's the "right" choice. She feels it, and that's enough.

This is why men, children, and even strangers respond to a woman who's in her feminine magnetism. Not because she says the right things, but because her presence tells the truth. She's not performing certainty. She is certainty. She's not trying to convince. She's already chosen. And people naturally calibrate to that.

You can still use logic as a tool, but let it follow the current of your energy, not lead it. Let logic serve your intuitive knowing, not silence it. Let it build the bridge only after the direction has been felt. Logic is there to support your path, not to replace your guidance system.

One of the simplest ways to shift out of logic and into feminine magnetism is to drop back into sensation. Ask yourself, What am I feeling in my body right now? Not what do I think about this situation, but what does my body say? Is there tightness? Expansion? A flutter in the chest or a pit in the stomach? These are not distractions from the truth. They are the truth. They speak before the words form. And they will never lie.

When a woman lives in this space consistently, she becomes magnetic because she becomes unpredictable in the best way. Not chaotic, but free. Her energy is not shaped by external logic, but by inner resonance. She doesn't manipulate or try to engineer an outcome. She aligns. And that alignment becomes its own gravitational force.

The most irresistible frequency you can hold is the frequency of a woman who trusts herself without needing permission, proof, or validation. That trust cannot be reasoned into existence. It is built by practice. By listening, feeling, and acting from the body. By choosing to value what is sensed over what is explained. And by returning, again and again, to the truth that your power does not come from how much you know, but from how deeply you trust what already knows you.

119

Let logic be your servant, not your queen. Let your magnetism rise not from cleverness, but from the courage to feel everything and still stand rooted in your own truth. That's the source of real power. And it cannot be argued with. It can only be felt.

Feminine Subconscious Reprogramming vs Masculine Affirmation Loops

There is a fundamental difference between how the masculine and the feminine create inner change. The masculine path relies on repetition, direction, and cognitive restructuring. The feminine path moves through the body, sensation, and symbolic integration. Both can create transformation, but they access different dimensions of the psyche, and they produce very different kinds of results.

Affirmation loops are a classic masculine tool. You choose a belief you want to embody, and you repeat it daily. "I am confident." "I attract abundance." "I am powerful." The idea is simple: say it enough, and your subconscious will eventually accept it. It's linear, structured, and rooted in the conscious mind directing the subconscious to obey. For some people, especially those whose inner world is already somewhat stable, this works. It reinforces an existing foundation.

But if your subconscious is holding onto deep emotional imprints, old stories, or unresolved traumas, affirmation loops can actually create more resistance. You might say, "I am safe," while your body is screaming that it's not. You might repeat, "I love myself," while your inner child is still frozen in a moment where she felt completely unworthy. The masculine method doesn't reach those parts. It stays at the surface, hoping repetition will drown out the deeper signals. But the feminine psyche doesn't respond to volume. It responds to resonance.

Feminine reprogramming works like water, not like fire. It doesn't bulldoze a new belief over an old one. It softens, surrounds, and gently dissolves the block at its root. This happens not through repetition, but through symbolic depth and somatic presence. You don't force a new thought into the mind. You create a new energetic experience in the body, and the subconscious naturally reorganizes around it.

This is why rituals, embodiment practices, sensual experiences, and dreamwork are far more effective for many women than logical self-talk. The feminine subconscious speaks a different language. It understands music, color, scent, memory, sensation, rhythm, archetype. It rewires through feeling, not phrasing. You could say an affirmation 100 times and never feel different. Or you could have one symbolic moment that shifts your entire relationship with yourself.

Think of the difference between telling yourself, "I am enough," and standing in front of a mirror, breathing into your womb, making soft eye contact with your own reflection, and letting your body say it without words. One is an instruction. The other is an invitation.

You can't trick your body into healing. You have to make it feel safe enough to let go. That's the essence of feminine reprogramming: it begins with safety, not force. If your nervous system doesn't feel safe with a new belief, it won't integrate it, no matter how many times you repeat it. But when you enter through the back door of sensation, emotion, and sacred slowness, the mind begins to shift without resistance. The new belief doesn't have to be argued into place. It just emerges as truth because the body finally believes it.

Letting go of the masculine way doesn't mean affirmations are wrong. It just means they must be used in a container that matches the feminine nervous system. A loop without embodiment is just noise. But when you speak an affirmation into your body after it has been softened, opened, and grounded, that phrase becomes a seed. And the womb knows how to grow it.

Feminine reprogramming requires presence, not pressure. When a woman brings her full awareness into her body, even without trying to fix anything, something begins to shift. This presence is not neutral or passive. It is deeply magnetic. It pulls truth from the shadows and offers it light without judgment. It is this gentle, yet potent, awareness that begins to unwind the false beliefs that have taken root beneath the surface.

You may notice that certain beliefs dissolve not because you mentally argue them away, but because you no longer feel them in your system. It's not that you convinced yourself you're worthy. It's that the cellular memory of unworthiness stopped vibrating inside you. The moment your body stops rehearsing the pain, your mind stops believing the lie. And this doesn't come from thinking. It comes from allowing.

The feminine approach also honors the nonlinear nature of true transformation. One day you may feel empowered and free, and the next you may feel tender, uncertain, or heavy. This isn't regression. It's integration. The subconscious is not a staircase you climb. It's a spiral you move through. Trying to force a belief into being every day can feel like failure when the emotional state doesn't match it. But when you work through feminine codes, you understand that every layer of emotion holds a message. You stop resisting your state and begin listening to it.

Sound, breath, and movement become essential tools. When you hum into your chest or pulse your hips slowly in rhythm with your breath, you aren't just engaging the body. You're speaking to the subconscious in its native language. This language does not respond to commands. It responds to reverence.

Reprogramming in this way is less about building something new and more about uncovering what's already there. Beneath the beliefs you picked up from childhood, culture, heartbreak, or fear, there is an ancient knowing. The feminine subconscious does not need to be filled. It needs to be remembered. That remembrance cannot happen in the noise of mental chatter. It happens in silence, in ritual, in the in-between spaces where logic has nothing left to say and feeling takes over.

This is why women who try to heal using purely mental tools often feel like they're hitting an invisible wall. The mind can only take you so far. It is the body that holds the codes. The more you drop into your body, the more you soften into presence, the more the reprogramming happens without effort. And what replaces the old belief isn't a perfect sentence. It's a new frequency. One that speaks through your energy, not your words.

If you truly want to embody a new identity, you cannot just repeat it. You have to feel what it's like to be her. Not in fantasy, but in vibration. What does she breathe like? How does she walk? What does her chest feel like when she sits in stillness? What choices would she no longer tolerate, not from anger, but from sovereignty? That's where the shift lives. In the sensations. In the inner posture. In the tiny moments that reshape who you are without ever needing to convince yourself.

Let the masculine model serve you when it fits. Use affirmations when your body is open and receptive. But let your main path be one of intimacy with your inner world. Let your subconscious rewire itself through touch, tone, texture, and timing. Let the symbols you surround yourself with do half the work. Let pleasure teach your nervous system it's safe to be alive again.

This is not about bypassing thought. It's about reclaiming the intelligence of feeling. True feminine reprogramming is not louder. It's deeper. And the more you trust that depth, the more life begins to rearrange itself around the woman you have always been underneath the noise.

Creating a Sensory-Based Reality Map That Bends Results

Most people live inside a mental blueprint of reality they never consciously chose. It's constructed from old conditioning, sensory memories, fragments of trauma, cultural programming, and inherited beliefs. But what if you could remap that internal landscape—not by forcing new thoughts, but by activating new sensations?

The subconscious does not operate in language. It understands rhythm, texture, scent, sound, temperature, and light. It is constantly updating your "reality map" based on sensory input. If you repeatedly feel cold, rushed, ignored, or depleted, your system internalizes that version of the world as normal. Without knowing it, you begin to orient toward experiences that match that emotional tone. You expect a certain level of chaos, lack, or hardness—and your nervous system filters out what doesn't match it.

To bend results in your life, you must begin not with outcomes, but with felt experience. Reality changes when your sensory system receives a new pattern consistently enough that it rewires what "normal" feels like. That shift must happen in the body first, not the mind.

The key is to start curating your sensory field with intention. Not to escape reality, but to overwrite it. Begin with the senses you ignore most. For many, that's touch. Think about how often you rush through your day without feeling the texture of your clothing, the pressure of your steps, the softness or sharpness of your environment. The body registers all of this, even when the mind does not. The more you tune in, the more you regain authorship over your internal world.

Touch becomes an anchoring tool. Wearing fabrics that feel sensual or powerful changes how your nervous system experiences the day. Sitting on furniture that makes your body soften, drinking from a cup that feels royal, lighting a candle with a scent that reminds you of intimacy or magic—these are not aesthetic choices. They are data points that your subconscious reads as part of your reality structure. Each one either reinforces the current map or begins to create a new one.

Sound plays a similar role. Your nervous system entrains to vibration. Environments filled with sharp, loud, or chaotic sound patterns create tension. But low, grounding tones, ambient frequencies, or silence recalibrate your system toward clarity. When you start your day with sound that matches the emotional tone of the results you desire, you begin training your body to expect those results—not intellectually, but energetically.

Smell is the shortcut few people use. The olfactory system is directly connected to memory and emotion. A specific scent can take you back to a childhood summer, a heartbreak, or a moment of power. You can use this to your advantage. Create a signature scent tied to a version of you that feels sovereign and magnetic. Breathe that in before any ritual, project, or encounter you want to imprint with new energy. Your body will begin to associate that frequency with who you're becoming.

Even temperature becomes a signal. If your world always feels cold, rushed, overstimulating, your subconscious learns that safety and ease are rare. But if you give yourself experiences that are warm, slow, and spacious—even for ten minutes a day—your system begins to register a new baseline. You don't just feel better in the moment. You start expecting the world to treat you differently.

This is not about controlling every sensory input. It's about using the tools you do have to shift the internal environment through which you interpret reality. Because the truth is, your subconscious doesn't care about your goals. It cares about familiarity. It will always choose the sensory world it knows over the one you want, unless you deliberately make the desired experience familiar. That's the only way to bend what shows up outside of you. By creating a new pattern inside you that feels more real than the one you inherited.

You don't need to wait for life to give you permission to shift the narrative. You only need to show your subconscious a new rhythm—repeatedly, consistently, patiently. This rhythm can be built through micro-signals. Small, consistent cues that bypass the rational mind and speak directly to the body. The way you breathe while making tea. The softness of your steps through your home. The lighting you choose when you read. All of these tell your system: *This is what life feels like now.*

If you want to experience more power, you must condition your body to recognize power as a baseline. That might look like slowing down your movements to signal control, or keeping your voice low and steady to register calm authority. When your nervous system lives in that rhythm, the outer world adjusts. People feel it before you speak. Situations respond to it before your mind catches up.

126

This is the essence of energetic leadership. You don't chase outcomes. You hold a specific sensory field long enough that reality begins to echo it. You become the gravitational center that pulls new dynamics into place.

The reason most people struggle with manifestation is not because they lack vision. It's because their internal environment is wired for contradiction. They say they want freedom, but their senses are soaked in tension. They say they want wealth, but their daily rituals reinforce lack. The subconscious gets confused. It defaults to the frequency it feels most often.

This is where feminine embodiment practices come in—not as aesthetic performances, but as direct access points to a new sensory identity. When you drop into your body, breathe through your belly, move with intention, surround yourself with beauty that nourishes rather than performs, you're not being frivolous. You're creating a new neurological and emotional map. You're telling the subconscious: *This is what reality feels like now. Match it.*
And it will.

Your job is not to micromanage the how. Your job is to anchor the frequency through every available sense. That's what opens the space for results to come in aligned form, often with more elegance and precision than your mind could have calculated. You shift from chasing to receiving. From controlling to embodying. From thinking to knowing.

Let the body teach the mind.

To fully activate this shift, you must become fiercely intentional about what you allow into your sensory space. Not with rigidity, but with reverence. Your environment is either expanding or constricting your power. Your home, your clothing, your rituals, your morning sounds, your evening light—all of it speaks to your subconscious. And your subconscious is always listening.

So instead of asking, "What do I need to do to get the result?" begin asking, "What would it feel like if that result were already here?" Then ask: "How can I feed that feeling into my body today, right now, with what I have?" The answer is often simpler than you think. A different scent. A slower breath. A texture that makes you feel chosen instead of tolerated.

You don't need to escape your life. You need to reshape the sensory pattern your life is wrapped in. This is the feminine way of bending reality. Not by force. Not by logic. But by presence, sensation, and frequency. The body becomes the altar. The senses become the doorway. And your lived

127

experience becomes the spell. One that rewrites not only how the world sees you, but how it shows up to meet you.

Chapter 11: Manifestation as Embodied Magnetism

Desire, Devotion, and Detachment: The Feminine Trinity

There is a rhythm that underlies all true feminine power. It doesn't chase. It doesn't rush. It doesn't grasp. And yet, it moves mountains, bends timelines, and calls in realities that logic alone could never touch. That rhythm is composed of three intertwined forces: desire, devotion, and detachment.

Most people only understand one or two of these, and even then, only through a fragmented lens. They think desire is need. That devotion is obsession. That detachment means not caring. But when fully embodied as a trinity, these forces become the energetic architecture of the magnetic feminine. They turn intention into reality, effortlessly.

Desire is the ignition. It's the sacred spark. But in a world that has pathologized women's wanting, desire often comes with shame. We're told to tone it down, to make ourselves easier to love, less intense, less hungry. As if craving more from life is an inconvenience. But in truth, desire is holy. It's the blueprint of your soul revealing what wants to unfold through you. Your desires are not random. They are directional. They are the compass pointing toward the life that is most aligned with your truth. To suppress them is to suppress your life force. But to honor them fully, without demand or desperation, is to awaken your magnetic field. Because what you deeply desire without clinging to becomes what you naturally attract.

Devotion is what gives desire roots. It is not about being attached to an outcome, a person, or a timeline. True devotion is about how you show up, how you hold your energy, how you become the space where what you desire feels safe to arrive. Devotion turns fleeting wants into embodied prayers.

A devoted woman doesn't just want something. She lives in a way that aligns with it. She becomes it before it ever appears. She chooses to cultivate beauty, presence, and integrity even when no one is watching. Even when the results seem far away. Because she knows: her field is being tuned. Her resonance is being clarified. And every moment of devotion is a declaration to the universe that she's ready to receive.

But here is where the third force becomes crucial. Without detachment, desire turns into need, and devotion becomes control. Detachment is not about giving up. It's about releasing the grip. It is the ability to let go of how, when, and in what form something must arrive. It is trusting that your energy speaks louder than your effort. That what is meant for you will not require self-abandonment to attain.

Detachment creates space for miracles. It opens the channel between your desire and its arrival. It removes the static of desperation, which is what often repels what we want most. Because when you need something in order to feel complete, you send a signal of lack. But when you can hold desire with reverence, show up with devotion, and still let go with trust, you become unstoppable.

Together, these three forces create an energetic spiral. Desire expands your field. Devotion anchors it. Detachment clears it. When these are in harmony, you no longer push or force. You magnetize. You move from trying to attract, to simply becoming the one who is already chosen. You collapse the distance between wanting and having, not because you chase the outcome, but because you become the version of you who already holds it with grace.

When you're living in full alignment with this trinity, you no longer wait for life to grant you permission. You give yourself permission to become the vibrational match to what you long for. And then, without forcing or rushing, life begins to mirror that decision back to you.

The woman who understands this doesn't walk into a room hoping to be chosen. She walks in already knowing she is the one. Not because she's arrogant. But because her energy is settled. Because her desire has been purified, her devotion embodied, and her detachment mastered. She is not seeking approval. She is signaling availability to only what honors her field.

The shift is subtle but profound. Most women have been taught to manifest by manipulating circumstances, over-efforting, or affirming endlessly from a place of mental rigidity. That is a masculine approach. It relies on mental willpower and control. But the feminine trinity doesn't work that way. It moves through embodiment, emotion, and energetic congruence. It doesn't chase. It aligns.

If you are constantly obsessing over whether it's working, whether it's close, whether you're doing enough, your field gets clouded. The signal weakens. This is where detachment becomes the healing force. To be unattached doesn't mean to be cold. It means your wholeness is no longer on the line. It means you can want something fully and still feel at peace if it takes time. You are no longer sourcing your identity from the result.

And that is the very thing that speeds it up. The moment your nervous system no longer signals lack, your field becomes magnetic. You shift from signaling "I hope it comes" to "I'm already living as her." That is the core of sacred feminine manifestation. It's not about deserving. It's about becoming.

There's also power in recognizing when these three forces are out of balance. When desire is overextended and becomes fantasy without any grounded devotion, it turns into constant craving. You become addicted to potential instead of rooted in reality. When devotion becomes obsession, you start performing for results instead of aligning with integrity. And when detachment becomes disconnection, you withdraw from your own desire and tell yourself you don't really want what your soul is clearly asking for.

The remedy is always returning to the center. Coming back to your body. Noticing how each of these forces feels when it's embodied properly. Desire feels expansive and exciting. Devotion feels grounding and nourishing. Detachment feels clear and light. If something starts to feel heavy, needy, or tense, you're being invited back into alignment.

The most powerful rituals are often the simplest. Sitting with your desire in silence. Asking yourself not just what you want, but why. Choosing daily practices that deepen your devotion to that vision without attaching to its timeline. Practicing letting go every night before sleep, telling life, "I trust you to deliver what is right, when it's right, without me having to grasp."

This trinity is not a performance. It's a frequency. The more you live from it, the more life opens in front of you. You stop needing constant proof. You stop collapsing every time there's silence. You learn to hold your desires with open hands, to walk with grace even when it's slow, and to bless the in-between rather than trying to escape it.

And perhaps most importantly, you begin to realize that the very embodiment of this energy is the reward. The feeling of being anchored in your power, at peace in your desire, and free in your surrender becomes more satisfying than anything outside of you could ever promise. You become the source. And once you are the source, nothing can truly be taken from you. Only reflected back.

Why You Attract Who You Are, Not What You Want

Desire is not the magnet. Identity is. You don't call in what you dream about. You call in what your nervous system believes is safe to hold. The life you experience isn't built on your conscious preferences. It's built on your unconscious agreements.

You can crave deep love, financial abundance, and emotional freedom. But if, deep in your body, you're still wired to expect betrayal, rejection, or scarcity, those cravings remain distant. Because energy doesn't respond to wishful thinking. It responds to the truth of who you're being.

This is where so many people get confused. They believe the strength of their desire should be enough to draw things in. They double down on vision boards, journals, and affirmations. But nothing seems to land. And they start to think something is wrong with them.

There's nothing wrong with the wanting. What's missing is the embodiment.

To manifest powerfully, you don't have to want harder. You have to become a match for the reality you're calling in. That's what makes it inevitable.

The universe doesn't deliver based on your words. It mirrors the dominant frequency of your being. If you're still operating from wounds, playing out unresolved patterns, or carrying shame and self-betrayal in your field, those energies speak louder than your goals.

Think of it like this: You can tell yourself "I'm ready for a healthy relationship," but if your energy still believes love is something to earn, you'll unconsciously be drawn to those who make you prove your worth. You can say "I'm calling in abundance," but if your subconscious still associates money with danger, chaos, or guilt, you'll repel it or sabotage it once it comes.

Attraction is energetic, not intellectual. And this is why surface-level tools often fall short. You can't trick life by saying the right things while embodying fear. You can't perform confidence while your body is locked in survival. You can't expect people to treat you with reverence while you chronically abandon your own needs.

What you're attracting is always an honest reflection of your most consistent state of being.

This is not punishment. It's precision. Life is responding to what you've normalized within. If chaos is familiar, peace might feel boring or unsafe. If emotional withdrawal is what you grew up with, intimacy might feel invasive. If you've lived with rejection, love might feel suspicious. So when we say, "you attract who you are," what we really mean is that your outer world mirrors your internal home.

Changing this isn't about faking a new persona. It's about rewriting the blueprint. It starts with radical honesty. Where in your life are you still leaking energy by settling, shrinking, or self-abandoning? What have you been tolerating that is not aligned with the woman you say you want to become?

This isn't about perfection. It's about coherence.

When your thoughts, actions, energy, and boundaries all align with your higher identity, you become magnetic. Not because you're doing more. But because your field becomes unmistakably clear. There is no split signal. No contradiction between your voice and your vibration.

And when the signal is clean, life doesn't hesitate.

You'll notice people treat you differently. Opportunities arrive without chasing. Invitations come from unexpected directions. Why? Because you're no longer trying to manipulate results from a fractured place. You're operating from wholeness.

Let's take this deeper.

The real work is not to force a new life into being, but to become the woman for whom that life is already natural. That means shedding identities built on fear, releasing narratives that keep you small, and correcting the subtle energetic postures of neediness, resentment, or lack that quietly shape your frequency.

You don't need to hustle for alignment. You need to stop rehearsing the identity of the woman who never gets what she wants.

This is why your healing is not just for your peace. It's also the foundation of your magnetism. When you shift from within, your presence changes before a word leaves your mouth. You walk into a room differently. You say "no" with clarity. You ask for what you desire without apology. And that vibration—clear, coherent, embodied—is impossible to ignore.

People pick up on it, even if they don't know why. They feel drawn to you, or intimidated by you, or intrigued in ways they can't explain. You're no longer broadcasting confusion or craving. You're emanating certainty. Not the kind that needs to be loud. The kind that lives in your bones.

And certainty is attractive. Not because it dominates. But because it creates safety. Safety in your standards. Safety in your energy. Safety in your self-respect. That kind of safety is what makes others lean in. Not because you're trying to pull them closer. But because they can finally feel a center that doesn't wobble.

This is why embodiment always trumps strategy. No amount of clever communication can override the energy of self-abandonment. No perfectly phrased message can mask the desperation underneath. But when your nervous system is regulated, your boundaries are embodied, and your identity is rooted in wholeness, you don't have to say much. Your field speaks for you.

The shift happens the moment you stop seeking worth through outcomes and decide you're already whole. The moment you stop trying to manipulate timing and surrender to the unfolding. The moment you stop chasing desire from lack and instead become the space where desire feels at home.

When you stop asking life to prove your worth and start living as if your worth is a settled fact, everything changes. Not overnight, not with fireworks, but with precision. People drop away. Others show up. Situations you used to tolerate become impossible to remain in. And the ones that match your new level start arriving without struggle.

This isn't magic. It's mechanics.

Your life bends around your identity. And identity is not built by repetition of thoughts. It's built by what you embody when no one is watching. By the standards you hold yourself to. By the way you treat your body, speak your truth, and trust your timing. By what you are willing to walk away from even when it scares you. That's the real magnetism. That's the real pull.

So ask yourself, gently but honestly: Who am I becoming when no one is clapping? Who am I choosing to be in silence, in the waiting, in the spaces where no outcome has landed yet? Because that is the woman your future is listening to. That is the self from which attraction flows.

You don't need to become louder, more likable, or more impressive. You only need to become more *true*. Strip away the noise. Release the performance. Return to the version of you who never needed to beg life for what was already hers. And from that place, watch what finds you. Not because you wanted it. But because you finally matched it.

Creating a Magnetic Field That Draws Without Effort

There is a difference between chasing what you desire and becoming the gravitational force that invites it. Most people have been taught to pursue outcomes, strategize their presence, and apply pressure until something gives way. But the feminine operates by an entirely different law. She doesn't pull with force. She *pulls with frequency*.

Magnetism is not about manipulation. It's not about wearing the right mask or saying the perfect thing. It's about being so aligned in your body, your truth, and your energy that life begins to move toward you—not because you pushed, but because you became the field in which those desires naturally unfold.

This field is built through coherence. When your inner world and outer expression are no longer at odds, you become energetically clean. There is no double signal, no subtle contradiction, no tension behind your smile. What you feel, what you believe, and what you communicate are one. And coherence is rare. That's why it stands out.

The moment you try to manufacture attraction by effort, you signal lack. Even if your words sound confident, the energy behind them betrays something else: need, desperation, performance. And need repels. It chokes the very current you're trying to activate. But when you don't *need*, when you simply *are*, your field becomes silent power. It whispers instead of shouting. It draws in instead of reaching out.

This is not to say magnetism requires stillness or passivity. It requires presence. It requires a rootedness in your own system that no external approval can shake. A kind of quiet sovereignty that makes others wonder what you know, what you've touched, and how they can get closer to it. Because they don't feel your reach. They feel your center.

Your magnetic field is shaped by what you embody consistently. If your nervous system is chronically dysregulated, if your boundaries are porous, if your desires are wrapped in fear, then your field will carry that dissonance. You may try to mask it with words or appearances, but people feel energy first. They always do. It's not logical. It's primal.

This is why regulating your energy is not optional. It is the foundation. And regulation doesn't mean becoming numb or emotionless. It means being able to hold your own charge. To stay in your body when things wobble.

To remain in alignment even when the external doesn't reflect your internal yet.

When your field becomes stable, you no longer try to *make things happen*. You become the place where things *want* to happen. Opportunities, people, ideas—they begin to orbit around you because your presence no longer emits resistance. You are not pushing against life. You are moving with it, but from the seat of your own power.

This energetic stance doesn't come from rehearsing positive thoughts. It comes from clearing the static. Releasing what doesn't belong. Letting go of the parts of you that learned to chase, to convince, to over-explain. It comes from creating safety inside yourself so that you no longer require it from others. That safety emits a frequency that is unmistakable. And that frequency? That's the draw.

Powerful magnetism requires containment. Not repression, but reverence. When your energy is scattered in trying to be seen, validated, or accepted, it bleeds out in all directions. You can have all the right intentions and still leak your influence if you're unconsciously performing for approval. Containment means you're no longer throwing energy outward hoping it lands somewhere. You hold your signal within yourself like a secret you don't need to explain.

This is the beginning of energetic refinement. You become aware of where your presence is going and whether it is being given or siphoned. You stop oversharing to prove your depth. You stop explaining to fix discomfort. You stop giving your essence to be chosen. Instead, you learn to savor your own presence first. That savoring generates a current. People feel it. They don't know what it is, but they want to be near it.

What most miss is that the field is created not when you want something, but when you trust yourself enough not to distort to get it. The distortion is the very thing that dilutes your power. You were magnetic before you became strategic. You were irresistible before you fragmented to fit someone else's lens. Your work is not to become magnetic. It's to unlearn the ways you abandoned the field that already lives in you.

This requires devotion to your own calibration. You must know what it feels like when you're fully in your body. When your words match your inner current. When your presence is quiet but undeniable. This is the kind of woman who enters a room and alters the atmosphere without needing to speak. Not because she is trying to command attention, but because she is not betraying her own frequency to get it.

The more you live in that alignment, the more your external life bends to accommodate it. Not instantly, not always comfortably, but inevitably. The field always wins over the surface. Energy always communicates faster than language. So when you become precise in your energy, when your yes and your no are clean, when your presence is undiluted by approval-seeking or self-abandonment, you become unforgettable. Not because of what you do, but because of what you carry.

This doesn't mean you never take action. It means your action arises from congruence, not from trying to prove your worth. It means your silence is as potent as your words. It means you're no longer auditioning for a life that you were meant to co-create through presence alone. Magnetism does not mean doing nothing. It means doing with intention, being with embodiment, choosing from clarity.

And when you're in this space, your life changes. The people who show up can feel the difference. They don't feel you reaching. They feel you holding. They don't sense pressure. They sense depth. Some will be pulled toward it. Others will be repelled by it. Both are signs that your field is working. Because magnetism is not about being liked. It's about being real. And realness, in a world addicted to performance, is power.

So the invitation is this: stop curating your image and start curating your energy. Become the space that things want to enter, not because you chased them down, but because you became the place where they feel safe to land. You don't need to sparkle to be chosen. You need to burn with the truth of who you are. That fire doesn't ask. It draws. Quietly. Powerfully. Effortlessly.

Chapter 12: The Ritual of Becoming

Designing Your Signature Daily Practice

A woman in her power does not stumble into alignment. She crafts it. Not rigidly, not with guilt or self-punishment, but as a sacred rhythm that holds her through the chaos of life. The daily practice is not about discipline in the traditional, masculine sense. It's about devotion. It's about choosing, again and again, to return to yourself before the world pulls you into its noise.

You are not meant to live in reaction. You are meant to move from a place of resonance. To do that, you need a space each day where you reconnect to your own inner frequency. This is where your power recalibrates. Where your nervous system softens. Where your intention aligns with your energy. This is not a chore. It is a ceremony.

A signature practice is not copied from a guru or pieced together from internet lists. It is built intuitively, intentionally, and sensually. It must feel like something you want to meet, not something you feel obligated to obey. If your practice feels like another thing on your to-do list, it's not the right practice for you. This is not about optimization. It's about anchoring.

There are days when the external world will feel louder than your truth. Days when you'll be tempted to respond to messages before responding to your body. Days when your thoughts will race ahead of your breath. That is exactly why you must have a practice that meets you where you are and brings you back to who you are.

This daily space is not about control. It's about remembrance. Remembering that you are a body before you are a brand. A breath before you are a task. A woman before you are a role. Without that daily remembering, the world will name you before you have the chance to name yourself. And once you've been named by the world, you begin to forget what it feels like to choose.

The dark feminine does not perform her power. She tends to it like a flame. Her daily practice is where that tending happens. Sometimes it is slow. Sometimes it is wild. Sometimes it is silent. But always, it is sacred. Even five minutes of deep, intentional presence can shift your entire field if done from truth.

Designing your own practice means listening. Not to the outside noise of what a spiritual morning *should* look like, but to the real needs of your own energy body. Do you need grounding? Expansion? Stillness? Movement? Do you need to weep or to shake or to breathe deeper into the space between your ribs? Your practice must reflect that.

There is no gold star for having a perfect ritual. There is only power in having a real one. One that you return to not because you fear what happens if you don't, but because you crave what happens when you do. That's what makes it magnetic. That's what makes it yours.

A practice that is deeply yours will begin to shape your reality in ways you cannot explain. You'll notice your days unfolding with more clarity, more calm, more precision. You'll say no without tension and yes without second-guessing. You'll find that the people and experiences that resonate with your truth start moving toward you effortlessly. Your life stops being a reaction to circumstance and becomes an expression of your inner alignment.

What makes a practice powerful is not its complexity but its intimacy. If you can't feel yourself inside it, it's not yours. And if it doesn't invite you back into your body, it will never anchor your energy in a way that transforms your field. So begin simply. Begin honestly. Begin by asking: *What brings me home to myself, without effort or performance?*

Sometimes that answer will be breath. Sometimes it will be sound. Sometimes it will be laying on the floor, hand over heart, eyes closed, whispering your name until your nervous system believes you again. The feminine does not need grand gestures. She needs presence. She needs you to stop abandoning her every time you reach for productivity before connection.

There is something deeply erotic about a woman who returns to herself each day, before returning to the world. That eroticism is not about sexuality. It's about intimacy with one's own essence. When you begin your day by tuning into your real needs, your real feelings, your real rhythm, you step into the world less fragmented and more sovereign. That is what makes you magnetic. Not the clothes, not the affirmations, not the rituals done from someone else's script. Your power is in your return.

The practice is not only about how you *start* your day. It is about how you *pattern* your day. Sacred pauses, moments of breath, check-ins with your inner world. You are not a machine to be optimized. You are a current that wants to flow. The more you interrupt the rush with stillness, the more your nervous system will stop perceiving life as a threat. This rewiring does not happen through logic. It happens through sensation.

Designing your daily practice means removing performance from the equation. You are not doing it to be good. You are not doing it to fix yourself. You are doing it to remember that you are already whole. The practice becomes a portal back to that knowing. Even when you forget. Especially when you forget.

If it helps you stay connected, assign a sensual anchor to your practice. A scent, a texture, a song. Something that reminds your body that this is *your* space. Not the world's. Not anyone else's. Yours. Let it become a cue for your nervous system to soften, your breath to deepen, your presence to return. Your signature practice must be a place you *want* to go. Not one you *should* go.

And if you miss a day? You start again, not from punishment but from devotion. You don't owe consistency to the outside world. You owe sacred space to yourself. That space is where your field realigns. Where your feminine recalibrates. Where your power deepens without effort, without explanation, and without external permission.

This is not about becoming a better version of yourself. It is about remembering the part of you that was never lost. That part needs tending, not taming. It needs reverence, not rules. Let your daily practice be the soft place where you meet that part of you and ask her what she wants. Then listen. Then move from her. That is the only alignment that will ever last.

Let your practice be your private revolution. A small, sacred defiance in a world that profits off your disconnection. Let it be the ritual that reclaims your wholeness. Not for validation. Not for praise. But because you finally decided that your own presence is worthy of your time. And once you decide that, everything else begins to orbit around your energy instead of pulling you away from it. That is the silent power of a woman in devotion to herself. That is how you become the source.

Integration Through Symbol, Sound, Movement, and Mirror Work

Transformation doesn't solidify through thought. It anchors through experience. The feminine path of becoming is not about accumulating more knowledge. It's about embodying the truths you've already touched. You may read, feel, and remember something profound — but until your body feels it, lives it, and expresses it without needing to explain it, that truth hasn't integrated. Integration is the final step of power. It is the moment knowledge turns into embodiment, and embodiment begins to shape reality. That kind of embodiment speaks a language older than logic. It speaks through symbol, sound, movement, and reflection. These are not random tools. They are primal technologies of the feminine, designed to bypass the analytical mind and communicate directly with the body and subconscious. You don't need to "understand" them in the way the intellect demands. You only need to experience them deeply, consistently, and with sacred intent.

Symbol as Portal

The feminine subconscious does not think in straight lines. It speaks in symbols, archetypes, images, colors, and sensations. When you work with symbols intentionally — whether through altars, sacred objects, art, or written sigils — you are planting messages in the soil of your inner world. These symbols act like seeds. You don't need to force them to grow. Your psyche will begin to rearrange itself around them, weaving them into your choices, desires, and behaviors.

Symbols also carry resonance. A specific symbol can carry generations of meaning and memory. When chosen with care, it becomes a living bridge between your conscious intent and your deeper knowing. That's why even a single object on your altar, if charged with intention, can hold more transformational power than a hundred affirmations. The symbol is not just a tool. It's a mirror of your inner world, externalized.

Sound as Frequency Alignment

You are not just flesh and thought. You are vibration. And vibration is shaped by sound. Your voice is not only for speaking. It is a tuning instrument. When you use your voice consciously — through breath, tone, chant, or hum — you are not just expressing emotion. You are reshaping the energetic field of your body. Your nervous system responds. Your cells respond. Even your emotions begin to soften or rise depending on the frequency you release.

This is why feminine practices often include toning, moaning, chanting, or humming. It's not performative. It's regulatory. Your voice becomes the medicine. When you sound from your belly, you drop out of performance and into presence. When you use sound to express what words cannot, the emotional body releases tension stored in places thought could never reach. You don't need to sing. You don't need to be loud. Even whispering your own name in a moment of dissociation can bring you back into your body. The sacred use of sound is less about how it *sounds* and more about how it *feels*. Let it feel raw. Let it feel strange. Let it feel honest. That's the frequency of recalibration.

Movement as Memory Rewriting

Your body holds the entire record of your lived experience. Every restriction, every opening, every pattern of tension or collapse — it's all data. And most of it is not stored in words. It lives in the fascia, the breath, the posture. Movement, then, becomes the key to rewriting memory. Not by changing the past, but by creating a new present where your body no longer has to hold the old story.

When you move with intention, you give the body permission to tell a new story without words. Whether it's sensual movement, shaking, dance, or simply swaying to music, you are giving your nervous system a new rhythm to inhabit. Movement is not performance. It is presence. It is a conversation between your now-body and your past-body, allowing the two to integrate through rhythm instead of reason.

The more you surrender to movement without needing it to look a certain way, the more your body begins to return to its original intelligence. There is a natural rhythm within you that knows how to release pain, express joy, and call in pleasure. That rhythm is not taught. It's remembered. And you remember it not by analyzing your posture, but by letting your hips circle when you're alone. By letting your shoulders melt without needing to control how you appear. By letting yourself feel where the contraction lives and meeting it with motion, not correction.

144

True integration happens when your body is no longer trying to protect you from the version of you that you used to be. Movement re-educates your system to trust life again, especially when it's slow, sensual, or primal. Especially when it has nothing to prove.

Mirror Work as Conscious Witnessing

The mirror can be one of the most confronting spiritual tools because it forces you to meet yourself without projection. It removes the buffer. You can't look away. You can't deflect. And in that space of direct seeing, the mirror becomes a powerful site of reprogramming. Not because it changes you, but because it reveals where you've abandoned yourself.

When you look into your own eyes without judgment, without makeup, without performance, something begins to shift. You're no longer just looking at your reflection. You're witnessing the woman who lived through what others never saw. The one who still shows up. The one who's been waiting to be acknowledged by you.

There is a sacred vulnerability in this practice. Saying to yourself, out loud, the words you longed to hear — even if your voice shakes. Telling yourself the truth you were taught to wait for someone else to say. The words that open you, that bring tears, that remind your inner child she's no longer alone. This is where the reprogramming happens, not through repetition, but through resonance.

The mirror doesn't lie. But it doesn't judge either. What you bring to it is what it reflects. When you bring reverence, it reflects worthiness. When you bring shame, it shows you the part that needs love. Not to fix it, but to feel it. Over time, mirror work becomes a ritual of devotion, not self-critique. You stop trying to perform beauty and begin to embody presence.

Letting the Integration Lead

There comes a point in your journey where you no longer need to think your way through transformation. You feel your way forward. The body tells you when it's safe to open. The nervous system reveals what needs to slow down. The voice rises when something must be claimed. The mirror calls you back when you forget your power. These are not separate tools. They are expressions of the same feminine language — the language of wholeness.

You do not need to master them all at once. Start with the one that calls you. Perhaps you place a single symbol near your bed and let it speak to you silently as you sleep. Perhaps you hum in the shower until your body remembers joy. Perhaps you dance in the dark until the shame begins to melt. Perhaps you stand in front of the mirror and, for the first time, say your own name with reverence.

Integration is not about doing more. It's about becoming more available to what already wants to move through you. The feminine doesn't force. She invites. She softens. She opens. And through that openness, she transforms everything she touches — not with pressure, but with presence.

This is where power is no longer a goal to chase. It becomes a frequency you return to. And when it lives in your symbols, your voice, your movement, and your reflection, it becomes unshakable. You don't need to convince anyone of who you are. You simply *are*. And that is more than enough.

Living As the Woman Who Already Has It

There is a shift that happens the moment you stop chasing the thing you desire and begin to embody the woman who already holds it. This is not about pretending or playing dress-up with the energy of what you want. It's about settling into a deeper truth. One where you recognize that desire is not something outside of you. It is something calling you home.

When you live as the woman who already has it, you stop negotiating with life. You no longer wait for permission to feel joy, sensuality, or freedom. You choose to inhabit the frequency now, because you understand that alignment is not a reward you earn, but a reality you step into. This is the essence of feminine manifestation: becoming the vessel that life responds to, not the beggar hoping for scraps of validation.

This version of you is not about performance. She is about presence. She walks differently, not because she's trying to be seen, but because she carries the weight of her own knowing. She makes decisions from desire, not from fear of loss. She moves from a deep inner yes that doesn't need justification. She chooses what supports her magnetism, not what proves her worth.

And most of all, she is no longer addicted to the timeline.

The woman who already has it doesn't rush. She doesn't constantly check if it's working. She knows that the more she settles into the frequency, the more life mirrors it back. Her job is to hold the field, to keep her body open, to keep her heart soft, to stay devoted to the version of her who already *is*. Everything else organizes itself around that.

The Embodiment of "Already"

To live from "already" means you no longer identify with the gap. You no longer speak about what you don't have in a way that makes it more real than your power. You stop reinforcing the absence and start cultivating the presence. The presence of wealth, even before the bank account reflects it. The presence of love, even before someone else names it. The presence of certainty, even in the face of external chaos.

This doesn't mean bypassing reality or denying current circumstances. It means understanding that circumstances are reflections, not definitions. You are not what is missing. You are what is remembering. And the more fully you remember your own capacity to create, the less you cling to what has not yet arrived.

This version of you knows how to hold the paradox. She can grieve and still walk in her power. She can be uncertain and still trust herself. She can feel the desire deeply without collapsing into lack. Because she understands that feeling is not the enemy. It is the doorway. And every time she steps into the feeling of already, even for a few moments, she reprograms her field.

There's a quiet rebellion in this. A refusal to play the game of "once I have it, then I'll be it." That game was never made for a woman like you. You don't need to earn your power. You simply need to claim it. Not through proving. Through being.

When you make decisions from that place, everything changes. The way you speak, the way you hold eye contact, the way you take up space, the way you receive. Your field becomes undeniable because it's rooted in truth, not strategy. And people feel it. Life feels it. There's a softness and a certainty that cannot be replicated or manipulated.

It is the frequency of inevitability.

There's nothing louder than the silence of a woman who knows. She doesn't have to announce her value. She doesn't chase opportunities. She simply stands in what she is, and the world reorganizes to meet her there. Her presence becomes the invitation. Her boundaries become her prayer. Her energy speaks before her words ever do.

This way of being isn't about control. It's about receptivity. Not the passive kind that waits and hopes, but the magnetic kind that draws, filters, and selects. She knows that the moment she sinks into the reality of "already," she activates a resonance that only matches what is aligned. Everything else naturally falls away. She doesn't have to fight for what's meant for her. She becomes the reason it shows up.

This is not wishful thinking dressed up in pretty language. It is a frequency discipline. It requires clarity, devotion, and the willingness to be misunderstood. You will not always be able to explain why you've stopped engaging the way you used to. Why you don't chase, overgive, or perform anymore. But you'll feel the difference in your nervous system. In your breath. In the weight that lifts when you realize you're no longer outsourcing your reality to people, timelines, or external proof.

She doesn't walk into the room wondering who will choose her. She chooses herself so completely that the room feels it. She doesn't need the thing she desires to confirm her worth. She lets her worth confirm the thing. That's the reversal. That's the power.

And she isn't trying to get everything right. She's not chasing perfection. She's playing with the moment. Letting life flirt with her. She's not worried about being liked or being too much. Her radiance doesn't ask for approval. It simply exists. She knows she doesn't need to do more to deserve more. She doesn't need to shrink or soften her voice to be palatable. She's not here to be digestible. She's here to be undeniable.

To live as the woman who already has it is to become unshakeable in your frequency. Not rigid, but anchored. Not guarded, but precise. You trust your intuition enough to let it guide your decisions without over-explaining them. You trust your energy enough to walk away from what doesn't feel right, even if it once did. And you trust your own embodiment enough to know that what is truly aligned doesn't require force. It arrives with clarity, with ease, with resonance.

There will be moments when your old self resurfaces. The one who wanted to prove, the one who feared being left behind. When that happens, you don't shame her. You don't suppress her. You hold her close and remind her that she's safe now. That she's no longer running the show. You let her rest, because the woman you are becoming has taken the lead.

This is the path of remembrance. Not of becoming someone new, but of returning to who you were before the world told you to forget. You are not chasing the version of you who has it all. You are dissolving everything that told you she didn't already live inside you.

And that is where true power begins.

Not in the things you achieve. Not in the outcomes you secure. But in the relationship you have with the now. In your ability to meet life without needing to bend it, twist it, or beg it to cooperate. You are not here to audition. You are here to embody. You are not here to earn. You are here to remember.

She already lives in you.

And the more you walk with her energy in your body, in your breath, in your choices, the more you realize: the woman who already has it never left. She was simply waiting for you to come home.

Last Words: Thank You

If you made it here, you didn't just read a book.
You moved energy. You unraveled illusions.
You remembered a part of yourself that was never broken, only buried.
This is not the end. It's a return.
To the woman you've always been beneath the conditioning, the pleasing, the waiting, the noise.
You don't need permission. You never did.
You are the source. You are the magnet.
You are the frequency that shifts the entire room without a word.
Thank you for walking this path with me.
Thank you for choosing yourself.
Thank you for becoming the woman who does not chase, beg, or shrink
— but simply *is*.
And from here forward...
Let everything come to you.
In devotion,

Elara Merritt

www.ingramcontent.com/pod-product-compliance
Lightning Source LLC
Chambersburg PA
CBHW072153270326
41930CB00011B/2403